PLEESECAKES

60 **AWESOME** NO-BAKE CHEESECAKE RECIPES

JOE MORUZZI
BRENDON PARRY

photography by Kris Kirkham

quadrille

Published in 2018 by Quadrille,
an imprint of Hardie Grant Publishing

Quadrille
52–54 Southwark Street
London SE1 1UN
quadrille.com

Cataloguing in Publication Data: a catalogue record for this
book is available from the British Library.

Text © Joe Moruzzi and Brendon Parry 2018
Photography © Kris Kirkham 2018
Design © Quadrille 2018

ISBN 978-1-78713-249-8

Printed in China

Publishing Director Sarah Lavelle
Project Editor Amy Christian
Art Direction and Design Claire Rochford
Photographer Kris Kirkham
Prop Stylist Louie Waller
Food Stylist Tamara Vos
Food Stylist's Assistant Maddy Montagu-Andrews
Production Controller Tom Moore
Production Director Vincent Smith

Contents

DEECE
decent/very good

choccy b
chocolate bar

DCB
double-choc base

GEEZERS
two guys who think they're the nuts

 hello

ABATT about

safe
bye

HOLDTIGHT listen up

EASY
hello

WHAT YOU SAYIN'?
how are you?

SWEET
good

BIG UP
not sure what it means but we say it a lot

INNIT
isn't it

you sweet?
you good?

GRAFT
hard work

HUH?
Huh?

WONGA money

EASE
hi

ALLOW IT
don't do that

wingin' it
doing something you ain't got a clue about

THIS BOOTS OFF
this is very successful

-PLEESE- -CAKES-

Holdtight! It wouldn't be a Pleesecake book without getting to know a bit about us geezers and the business, would it? Even writing these first few words of the book makes us laugh.

painters AND DECORATORS **DON'T WRITE BOOKS!**

yet here we are – writing a book!

We're two friends who went to school together then ended up crossing paths again in our early twenties. Joe was busy doing all types of graft, from landscaping to bar work. Brendon left school and just painted and painted away until one day Joe started working for Brendon with his first company (Bren-Dec). That went pear-shaped and PARMOR contractors was born. We ran that painting and decorating company together for three years – luxury homes and blocks of 40 apartments were our day-to-dayer!

We were foodies from birth: Brendon makes a banging homemade sausage roll and gives them out at Christmas instead of presents! And Joe was randomly making these cheesecakes. We knew that one day we'd end up doing something with food in some way …

Three years ago, Joe's dad, known to many as 'Gian' or 'Jon', attempted to make a cheesecake. Unbeknown to any of us he was amazingly not so great at it. Joe proceeded to have a go at it. Unbeknown to any of us, he was amazingly not so great at it!

It took a further two years to get to a stage where he felt people would pay their hard-earned wonga for one of his creations. He practised a lot, watched videos on Instagram and kept trying new ways and techniques to make the cheesecake look much more enticing than your boring, generic, baked New York style! He was on a mission to reinvent the cheesecake! Wend (Joe's old dear) stepped in as sous chef and would be on call whenever he entered the kitchen! She has since stepped down, but Joe will be forever grateful. She has since moved on to bigger and better things – as the Pleesecakes delivery driver!

Rubbing down skirtings and rolling ceilings by day, putting pretty little raspberries and gold chocolates on cakes by night – that was the routine! Food was Joe's passion, but cakes weren't a geezer thing to do. People loved them though, and it was an obvious thing to pursue.

Enter Brendon (aka 'Brenchef'/'Brendec'), business partner and double-keen foodie. He was a clear choice to help drive this hobby into something big (and Joe needed someone to wash up)! Plus, his knees were sore from rubbing down untold skirtings.

On 3 January 2017 the Pleesecake Instagram account was set up. We got a shout-out from Joe Wicks (The Body Coach) and boom – 10k followers in 24 hours! A business is born and Pleesecakes is abaatttt on the scene.

We met in a cafe in Epsom the following morning and realized we had to do something with this! So we set up a website and email. We had 50 orders within hours. We were looking at renting shops and kitchen spaces within two weeks of launch as we were still using Brendon's two bedroom maisonette for the entire operation. It was a shock to us, as well as our wives, girlfriends, friends and family, who didn't know what was happening!

Since the birth of Pleesecakes there have been highs, lows, early mornings and late nights. A standard day would be a 12-hour shift ,and a long day could be a dutty 20-hour shift. We didn't realize the amount of work and struggle that goes into growing a business. Yes, we'd had experience from our previous business but scaling a business in an industry in which you have zero experience or expertise was a challenge to say the least! Making mistakes was a daily/hourly occurrence. We had to learn quick, REAL QUICK!

We hope that this book will inspire you. Chase your passion in life, because doing something for a large proportion of your time that you're not passionate about is a waste of life! Our main focus is on creating experiences and memories through making and eating good, healthy and indulgent food, specifically in the many different flavours, shapes and sizes of a cheesecake!

brendon
the KP

joe
the master decorator/creator

Now get involved ...

Equipment

You don't really need any specialist equipment – we really wanted to make this book accessible. At the end of the day we're just two painters who have found equipment along the way that is useful for us. When we first started out, we used to use an old plastic vitamin-C pot to press down the biscuit base into the tin! You can also use a cup or tumbler.

The standard sharing Pleesecake recipes in this book are made in springform cake tins (pans) of different sizes (below). These can be bought in any supermarket or cook shop.

The individual Pleesecakes are made in mini cheesecake moulds or a mini cheesecake tray with 12 compartments (see opposite). These are available to buy online. You can also get smaller mini cheesecake trays, which have 20 compartments. These are handy for making bitesize party Pleesecakes. Ring cutters in a range of different sizes can also be useful. A set of measuring cups are helpful for measuring out the biscuit base, and palette knives for smoothing out toppings.

You might have realized already that this is not your standard cheesecake book, and we've got recipes made in loaf tins, teacups, tumblers, martini glasses, champagne flutes and even shot glasses! So get creative and use whatever you fancy …

BASE
+
FILLING
+
TOPPING
=
pleesecake heaven

Choose your size and grab your tin, mould, tray or glass (see page 14).

Base
Biscuit crumbs and melted butter are mixed together with any flavourings then pressed into the mould.

Filling
A cream cheese and sugar mix is the backbone of our Pleesecakes. Add whatever flavours you like here. Whip cream into stiff peaks, mix it all together, then spoon on top of the base.

Once your cheesecake mix is in your tin (pan), give it a tap a few times on the kitchen worktop, this will get the air bubbles out and make sure your cheesecake mix is nice and even around that biscuit base.

Freeze the base and filling to make it nice and easy to get your Pleesecake out of the mould. A solid base makes piling on those toppings easier, too.

Toppings
This is where you can really get creative. Drizzle over chocolate sauce, or pile up fruit, sweets or chocolate bars. Check out our Insta for inspiration. Just remember – pile it up nice and high!

cheesecake heaven

= TOPPING

+ FILLING

+ BASE

ALPACINO
CAPPUCCINO

BREAKFAST
POTS

pancakes

fluffy

**BANANA &
MARMITE
MINIS**

FULL ENGLISH
IN A MUG

H
P

matcha tea minis

SIZZLING BACON
& MAPLE SYRUP
MINIS

ALTHY
NCAKES

BREAKFAST POTS

Believe it or not, we try to eat healthily as much as we can. So, to reduce the circumference of our ever-expanding Derby Kellys (bellies), we sack the full English off at least five days a week and replace it with something that our bodies might actually be thankful for. Don't get us wrong though, there is a bit of guilt in this recipe, because frankly life's too bloody short! Quick and simple – if you have a double busy life, this one's got your back.

We're looking for speed on this one, so grab the nearest serving vessel – a mug, bowl or wine glass – and add your granola of choice to create a structurally sound foundation.

Mix together the Greek yogurt, mascarpone cheese and cinnamon, and cover the granola base evenly.

To make this a little more interesting, get some banging mixed-berry compote (none of that cheap stuff!) and spoon on a healthy dollop. Add a little handful of dried fruit, some pine nuts, a drizzle of honey and a dusting of cinnamon, and you're ready to tuck in and get the boost of energy you need before setting off for a day's graft!

You'll need: 2 serving bowls

Base
100g (1 cup) granola

Filling
140g ($^2/_3$ cup) Greek yogurt
125g (generous $^1/_2$ cup)
  mascarpone cheese
$^1/_4$ tsp ground cinnamon

Topping
2 tbsp mixed berry compote
2 tbsp dried fruit
2 tbsp pine nuts
2 tbsp honey
$^1/_4$ tsp ground cinnamon

Serves 👤👤

ALPACINO CAPPUCCINO

The cappuccino has been a good friend of ours for many years now. When you've got a cold, early start and you're walking on to a building site with 16 ceilings to roller, you need a little kick to get you going. Plus, the way we've constructed this one, it's a looker, so it's not just the punchy flavours that are going to impress people.

Let's go. Whizz the biscotti biscuits to a chunky crumb in a food processor (stick 'em in a sandwich bag and bash with a rolling pin if you haven't got a processor). Divide them evenly between the teacups (40g/1½oz per serving), press down gently to make your base and set aside.

Get your cream cheese, espresso shots and caster sugar (you can adjust the amount to taste, depending on how sweet you like your coffee) into a mixing bowl and beat together until silky smooth and golden in colour. Whip the cream until you have stiff peaks and fold it gently into the mix. Spoon into the cups and level off with a palette knife. Stick 'em in the fridge for at least 2 hours to set.

For the topping of Italian meringue, lightly whisk the egg whites and the cream of tartar. Put the sugar and water into a saucepan and bring to the boil. Let it boil, removing from the heat when the temperature hits 118°C (245°F).

Pour the sugar syrup into the lightly whisked egg whites, while whisking at a high speed to encourage cooling. You don't want scrambled eggs, so keep an eye on it. You're looking for firm peaks, and a silky, shiny finish.

Once the filling has set, spoon – or, if you're feeling like Gordon Ramsay, pipe – meringue mix into each cup. Give it a blast with a blow torch or under the grill (broiler) for a minute, sprinkle with cocoa powder and you have just made a banging little dessert. Well done, give yourself a pat on the back!

You'll need: 2 glass teacups

Base
80g (2¾oz) biscotti biscuits

Filling
90g (scant ½ cup) cream cheese
2 shots espresso
50g (¼ cup) caster (superfine) sugar
30ml (2 tbsp) double (heavy) cream

Topping
3 large eggs, separated
5g (1½ tsp) cream of tartar
150g (¾ cup) caster (superfine) sugar
75ml (scant ⅓ cup) water
cocoa powder, for sprinkling

Serves 👤👤

MATCHA TEA MINIS

Matcha is a bit quirky for us ex-painter and decorators, but we're telling you now that you are in for a treat. These matcha minis are simple and light, and a nice contrast to some of the other recipes in this book. They're not only for breakfast – if you've had a heavy meal and you want something light and refreshing to take the edge off things, give these a go – you won't be disappointed. Double simple, double nice!

Right, let's get started. Whizz the digestive biscuits to a fine crumb in a food processor (stick 'em in a sandwich bag and bash with a rolling pin if you haven't got a processor). Add the melted butter and give it a good stir to make sure that all the biscuit is nicely coated in butter, then mix in the white chocolate drops. Divide evenly between the moulds, press down gently to make your base and place in the freezer for 15 minutes to firm up.

Beat the cream cheese and sugar together. Add the matcha powder and mix together thoroughly. Whip the cream until you have stiff peaks and fold it gently into the mix. Spoon into the moulds and level off with a palette knife. Stick 'em back in the freezer for at least 2 hours to set.

Once set, remove from the freezer and take them out of the moulds. For the decoration, blitz the digestive biscuit to a fine crumb and sprinkle a little on each cake, followed by the matcha powder. Decorate with a few white choc drops and a drizzle of cream, if you like. Job done.

Allow to defrost in the fridge for 1–2 hours before serving.

You'll need: 2 mini cheesecake moulds or a mini cheesecake tray (12 compartments)

Base
60g (2¼oz) plain digestive biscuits
20g (1½ tbsp) unsalted butter, melted
2 tbsp white chocolate drops

Filling
240g (generous 1 cup) cream cheese
80g (generous ⅓ cup) caster (superfine) sugar
1 tsp matcha tea powder
80ml (⅓ cup) double (heavy) cream

Topping
1 plain digestive biscuit
2g (½ tsp) matcha tea powder
1 ¼ tbsp white chocolate drops
5ml (1 tsp) double (heavy) cream (optional)

Serves 🧍🧍

CHEESECAKE IS AN EXPERIENCE

We used to go to various eateries, and there would normally be a cheesecake in the dessert section.

Borrrrrinnngggg

They were always so samey, with no character; sure they tasted OK, but we wanted to bring personality to them. There's a lot of love for cheesecake, more than we ever realized. The amount of people that we used to speak to who said, we hate cake, but we love cheesecake was exciting to hear because it was a turning point – we found out that we weren't the only ones who loved cheesecake! A cheesecake can be so social, bringing friends and family together even without an occasion to celebrate. We wanted to reinvent the cheesecake and make it a memorable experience.

GUILTYYYY PANCAKES

Boy, oh boy, this recipe has got to be one of our favourites. It's the ultimate cheat pudding. We've always been into capping a meal off with a double naughty dessert, and after you've tried these beautiful indulgent guilty pancakes, you ain't going to be looking any further. If you want to show off to your missus, fella, dog, cat or hamster be sure to make these for them, you'll have them eating out of your hands in no time. See page 30 for a healthier version!

Right, let's get this pancake party booting off. To make the filling, beat the cream cheese and sugar together. Add the chocolate hazelnut spread and vanilla extract to the cream cheese and mix together thoroughly. Whip the cream until you have stiff peaks and fold it gently into the mix. Add the chocolate chips and marshmallows and stir through the mix. Put to one side.

For the pancakes, in a bowl, sift together the flour, bicarbonate of soda (baking soda), salt and sugar. In a separate bowl, mix together the buttermilk, milk, eggs and butter. Pour the egg and milk mixture into the flour bowl and whisk together, then stir in the marshmallows and the chocolate chips.

Melt a knob of butter in a frying pan set over a medium heat. Ladle the batter into the frying pan, making a small pancake puddle. Cook the pancake for 1–2 minutes per side. Repeat for each pancake.

Now for the fun part! There ain't no right or wrong here but you can see how we constructed ours in the picture opposite. Stack them how you want but just promise us that you won't hold back! Make them double guilty and double naughty. These are best enjoyed warm and straight from the pan, so don't waste any time! Get going!

Serves 🧍🧍🧍🧍🧍🧍

Pancakes
350g (2²/₃ cups) self-raising (self-rising) flour
1 tsp bicarbonate of soda (baking soda)
¹/₂ tsp salt
40g (scant ¹/₄ cup) caster (superfine) sugar
200ml (generous ³/₄ cup) buttermilk
400ml (scant 1²/₃ cups) semi-skimmed (reduced fat 2%) milk
2 eggs
25g (¹/₂ tbsp) butter, melted, plus extra to fry
60g (1¹/₂ cups) mini marshmallows
60g (¹/₃ cup) chocolate chips

Filling
420g (15oz) cream cheese
40g (scant ¹/₄ cup) caster (superfine) sugar
180g (scant ²/₃ cup) chocolate hazelnut spread
10ml (2 tsp) vanilla extract
240ml (1 cup) double (heavy) cream
60g (¹/₃ cup) chocolate chips
60g (1¹/₂ cups) mini marshmallows

Toppings
100g (generous ¹/₃ cup) chocolate sauce
100g (²/₃ cup) chocolate chips
50g (1 cup) mini marshmallows

HEALTHY PANCAKES

Life's all about balance, ay?! If you fancy some pancakes but don't want an all-out blowout, give these bad boys a go. They are banging and great for breakfast (obviously), as a pre- or post-workout meal or – if you're like us – whenever you want. They're double decent!

Right, let's get going. You want to stick your banana, protein powder and egg into a blender and whizz it all up into a smooth batter.

Mix your yogurt and cream cheese together. This is the filling that will be stacked up in between your pancakes – for now, set aside.

Get your frying pan over a medium heat and melt the coconut oil. Pour a quarter of the batter into the frying pan (you should get four pancakes out of the mix), and fry on both sides for a minute. Once golden brown, put your first pancake on a plate and cook a second pancake to go on a second plate. When these bottom-layer pancakes are cool, whack some of your filling mixture on top, drizzle with some honey and sprinkle with some blueberries and chia seeds. Then continue cooking the final two pancakes, piling them on top and finishing off with some filling mix again.

To top, we suggest some raspberries, a little more honey and a zesting of orange. But there ain't no right or wrong with this, so you can construct them how you like. Just be creative and make sure you enjoy. Now crack on.

Pancakes
140g (5oz) banana
35g (1¼oz) whey protein
1 large egg
1 tsp coconut oil, for frying

Filling
100g (½ cup) Greek yogurt
100g (scant ½ cup) low-fat cream
  cheese
2 tbsp honey
100g (¾ cup) blueberries
30g (3 tbsp) chia seeds

Topping
40g (⅓ cup) raspberries
2 tsp honey
zest of ½ orange

Serves 👤👤

FULL ENGLISH IN A MUG

You can't beat a good old Full English. This recipe is quality, bang it all in a mug and enjoy it in bed on a Saturday morning with your missus or fella. Give it a go – it's a proper win!

Preheat your oven to 200°C (400°F/gas mark 6). Start by grating the potatoes and onion. Squeeze as much of the liquid as you can out of the grated potato to make it super-dry for cooking. Crack an egg, give it a whisk and bung it in the potato and onion mix with a pinch of salt and pepper, and mix it up. Then smash it on an oiled baking tray, spreading it out fairly evenly about 1.5cm (½ inch) thick. Whack it in the oven for about 25 minutes. You want a crispy outer and a fluffy inner for your hash brown!

Now cook your toppings. Sausages will take about 20 minutes in the oven. Stick your bacon in with the sausages (depends how crispy you like your bacon, so you can be the judge of how long for). Then it's time to get some proper flavour players involved. Add the black pud, mushrooms and tomatoes for the last 10 minutes of cooking – same tray as the sausages and bacon, we ain't messing around now!

With 5 minutes to go, put your beans in a saucepan, give 'em a good old season with salt and pepper, and gently bring them to a simmer. Throw in a handful of your favourite cheese (has to be a mature Cheddar) and let the magic commence! The beans will go all silky and gooey – when that happens, you know you've scored decent points with your other half! Take them off the heat and put to one side.

Chuck a couple of quail's eggs in a saucepan of boiling water and soft-boil for 2–2½ minutes. Get 'em off the heat and under some cold water.

Right, your timer's gone off on the oven, so you're now ready to construct this guv'nor of a breakfast. Divide your hash brown into two and create a base at the bottom of each mug, then pour your cheesy beans in, leaving enough room for your other bits. Whack your sausages, bacon, black pud, mushrooms, cherry toms and egg on top of your beans, then add watercress or parsley. Get some nice crusty toast on ya plate, cuppa Rosie Lee (tea) and wallop, you're done – a Full-English inspired Pleesecake in a mug.

You'll need: 2 glass mugs

Base
2 medium potatoes
1 medium onion
1 egg
2 tbsp olive oil
salt and pepper

Filling
350g (1⅓ cups) baked beans
100g (3½oz) mature Cheddar cheese
salt and pepper

Topping
2 chipolata sausages
4 streaky bacon rashers (slices) (smoked is guilty)
4 black pudding slices (optional)
50g (1¾oz) button mushrooms
4 on-the-vine cherry tomatoes
2 quail's eggs
sprigs of watercress or parsley
buttered toast, to serve

Serves

SIZZLING BACON & MAPLE SYRUP MINIS

Right, hear us out – this may not sound like a good flavour combination but, cor blimey, it boots off! The sweet maple syrup and the salty bacon give you a proper party mouth! On paper, this doesn't work, but off paper IT WORKS! (Well, we think it does.) We've both ventured over to the USA a few times and each time we've realized that there's just no point to your trip if you don't indulge in pancakes, bacon and maple syrup for breakfast at least once. So that's the inspiration. Everything we eat these days, we question whether we can turn it into a cheesecake somehow. This one passed extensive taste tests.

Let's get going by whacking the bacon for both the base and filling into a preheated oven (200°C/400°F/gas mark 6) for 6–8 minutes.

While the bacon is sizzling, whizz the digestive biscuits to a fine crumb in a food processor (stick 'em in a sandwich bag and bash with a rolling pin if you haven't got a processor). Add the melted butter, and give it a good stir to make sure that all the biscuit is nicely coated in butter. When the bacon is nice and crispy, remove from the oven and let it cool, then chop it up finely. Add half to the biscuit mix and stir well. Divide evenly between the moulds, press down gently to form the base and place in the fridge for 30 minutes to firm up.

Beat the cream cheese and sugar together. Add the remaining chopped crispy bacon to the mix, along with the maple syrup, and mix together thoroughly. Whip the cream until you have soft peaks and fold it gently into the mix. Spoon into the moulds and level off with a palette knife. Throw them into the fridge (not literally) for at least 2 hours to set.

Once set, remove from the fridge and take them out of the moulds. To serve, whack some more beautiful crispy bacon (sizzling fresh from the oven, ideally) on top and finish with a drizzle of maple syrup. This is a real 'don't knock it until you try it' dish!

You'll need: 2 mini cheesecake moulds or a mini cheesecake tray (12 compartments)

Base
10g (¼oz) streaky (fatty) bacon
60g (2¼oz) plain digestive biscuits
20g (1½ tbsp) unsalted butter, melted

Filling
10g (¼oz) streaky (fatty) bacon
200g (scant 1 cup) cream cheese
40g (scant ¼ cup) caster (superfine) sugar
1 tbsp maple syrup
80ml (⅓ cup) double (heavy) cream

Topping
4 streaky (fatty) bacon rashers (slices)
1 tbsp maple syrup

Serves

BANANA & MARMITE MINIS

We've had some unusual requests from customers, and this is one of them. We like to give our customers free reign to decide what flavours they want in their Pleesecake, but we were taken aback by this one. We thought, this ain't gonna work. Not sure if you've ever had cheese and Marmite on toast – pretty decent! Why not add some banana into the mix? Believe us when we say this combination works! If you're looking for something a little different, give this a blast!

Start by whizzing the biscuits to a fine crumb in a food processor (stick 'em in a sandwich bag and bash with a rolling pin if you haven't got a processor). Add the melted butter, and give it a good stir to make sure that all the biscuit is nicely coated in butter. Roughly chop half the banana chips and mix them into the biscuits. Divide evenly between the moulds, press down gently to make your base and place in the fridge for 30 minutes to firm up.

Beat the cream cheese and sugar together. Add the banana essence and the mashed banana and mix together thoroughly. Whip the cream until you have stiff peaks and fold it gently into the mix. Lastly, spoon in the Marmite and lightly stir it in, creating a marbled effect.

Spoon into the moulds and level off with a palette knife. Whack them back in the fridge for at least 2 hours to set.

Once set, remove from the fridge and take them out of the moulds. To top, start by chopping the banana into chunks. Sprinkle the banana with the sugar. Now, if you're feeling all chefy, caramelize the bananas using a small blow torch, or just whack them under the grill (broiler) for a couple of minutes until golden brown. Now bung them on top of the cheesecakes, along with the rest of the banana chips and a final drizzle of Marmite.

BANG! You're either going to love it or hate it.

You'll need: 2 mini cheesecake moulds or a mini cheesecake tray (12 compartments)

Base
60g (2$\frac{1}{4}$oz) plain digestive biscuits
20g (1$\frac{1}{2}$ tbsp) unsalted butter, melted
20g ($\frac{1}{3}$ cup) dried banana chips

Filling
180g (generous $\frac{3}{4}$ cup) cream cheese
40g (scant $\frac{1}{4}$ cup) soft brown sugar
8 drops banana essence
90g (3$\frac{1}{4}$ oz) banana, mashed
80ml ($\frac{1}{3}$ cup) double (heavy) cream
30g (1$\frac{2}{3}$ tbsp) Marmite or other yeast extract

Topping
70g (2$\frac{1}{2}$oz) fresh banana
15g (1$\frac{1}{4}$ tbsp) caster (superfine) sugar
10g ($\frac{1}{2}$ tbsp) Marmite or other yeast extract

Serves

ALMOND & ORANGE CAKE

CHOC SALTED
CARAMEL
NICEY SLICEY

COCONUT & CHOCOLATE LAYER CAKE

cookies & cream sandwich

CHOC

AVOCADO & DARK CHOCOLATE MINIS

ORANGE POPCORN

lemon & AVOCADO & LIME
raspberry minis

GUILT-FREE
SUMMER FRUIT
PLEESECAKE

PROTEIN
SLICES

NIS

We're not all about sugar and the C word **(calories)** over at Pleesecakes!

We all need balance in our diet. Believe it or not, we were both signed up to do an Iron Man triathlon in July 2017, which consists of a 2.4-mile swim, a 112-mile cycle and, to finish, a full-distance marathon. Unfortunately, or possibly fortunately (!), Pleesecakes took off so much we had to commit ourselves to the cheesecake world and postpone until further notice. But we did start training and while you're training,

you just can't smash cheesecake as an energy source

– which is why we have various healthier options that are a better source of energy but still taste great!

AVOCADO & LIME MINIS

We use avocado quite a bit, mainly because we like it and it tastes great with so many other things. Even though avocado is really good for you, this recipe is a full-on guilty one, but with the zingy lime it's worth all that guilt! Tastes so decent!

Whizz the biscuits to a fine crumb in a food processor (stick 'em in a sandwich bag and bash with a rolling pin if you haven't got a processor). Add the melted butter and give it a good stir to make sure that all the biscuit is nicely coated, then mix in the choc drops. Divide evenly between the moulds, press down gently to make your base and place in the freezer for 15 minutes to firm up.

Beat the cream cheese and sugar together. Mash up the avocado in a separate bowl, making sure it's nice and smooth. Add to the cream cheese along with the lime zest and juice, and mix together thoroughly. Whip the cream until you have stiff peaks, and fold it gently into the mix. Spoon into the moulds and level off with a palette knife. Stick 'em back in the freezer for at least 2 hours to set.

Once set, remove from the freezer and take them out of the moulds. Melt the chocolate in the microwave or a heatproof bowl set over a pan of simmering water, then drizzle over each cake. A zesting of lime and these are finished!

Allow to defrost in the fridge for 1–2 hours before serving.

You'll need: 3 mini cheesecake moulds or a mini cheesecake tray (12 compartments)

Base
120g (4¼oz) double chocolate digestive biscuits
15g (1 tbsp) unsalted butter, melted
3 tbsp dark chocolate drops

Filling
175g (¾ cup) cream cheese
25g (2 tbsp) caster (superfine) sugar
200g (7oz) avocado flesh (very ripe is best)
zest and juice of 3 limes
90ml (generous ⅓ cup) double (heavy) cream

Topping
120g (4¼oz) dark chocolate
zest of ½ lime

Serves 👤👤👤

PROTEIN SLICES

Holdtight gym fans! These protein slices are decent for all you six-pack-seeking geezers and bikini-bod sorts if you're trying to keep the old sweet tooth on lockdown until you reach your gym-bod goal. They can be made in batches, so get 'em done, get 'em made and stock that freezer up – like the Body Coach says, prep like a boss.

Let's start by getting the base made. Melt the coconut oil in the microwave for about 30 seconds. Add the coconut, protein powder, cacao powder and ground walnuts to the bowl and mix together well until all the ingredients are nicely coated in oil. Divide evenly between the mini loaf tins, press down gently to make your base and place in the freezer for 15 minutes to firm up.

Let's get the filling done now. Get a clean bowl and throw in your cream cheese, yogurt, protein powder and dark choc chips, and mix all really well together. Spoon into the moulds and level off with a palette knife. Stick 'em back in the freezer for at least 2 hours to set.

Once set, remove from the freezer, take them out of the moulds and they're ready for decorating. Melt the chocolate with the coconut oil in the microwave (or in a heatproof bowl set over a pan of simmering water) until silky smooth with no lumps. Drizzle each slice evenly using a spoon and top with a sprinkle of coconut, some crushed hazelnuts and the dark choc chips. Boom! There you have it, another naughty-looking but double-nice cheesecake. Big up.

Allow to defrost in the fridge for 1–2 hours before serving.

You'll need: 4 mini loaf tins with loose bottoms

Base
25g (2 tbsp) coconut oil
30g (¹⁄₃ cup) desiccated (shredded) coconut
35g (1¹⁄₄oz) whey protein powder
5g (1 tbsp) cacao powder
60g (³⁄₄ cup) ground walnuts

Filling
180g (³⁄₄ cup) light cream cheese
90g (¹⁄₃ cup) 0% Greek yogurt
75g (2³⁄₄oz) whey protein powder
20g (2 tbsp) dark chocolate chips

Topping
50g (1³⁄₄oz) dark chocolate
5g (1 tsp) coconut oil
5g (1 tbsp) desiccated (shredded) coconut
8g (1 tbsp) hazelnuts, crushed
5g (¹⁄₂ tbsp) dark chocolate chips

Serves

CHOC SALTED CARAMEL NICEY SLICEY

I guarantee you'll be able to convert the most anti-vegan person you know with these! Make a big batch and whack 'em in your freezer.

Grease the cake tin (pan) and stick the kettle on. Soak those cashew nuts in boiling water for at least an hour – preferably overnight. Soak your dates in boiling water for 10 minutes.

While the dates are soaking, whizz the walnuts and chocolate to a semi-coarse texture in a food processor. Strain the dates into a sieve and squeeze out the excess water. Throw the dates, walnuts, chocolate, tahini (sesame) and cacao powder into a bowl and mash them with your hands, until the dates have broken down and the mixture binds together. Grab your cake tin and spread the base mixture evenly across the bottom with the back of your hand. Whack it in the freezer for 15 minutes while you crack on with the rest.

Now it's time for the filling! Drain the cashews (making sure they're soft), then chuck them into a food processor, along with the coconut milk, maple syrup, almond milk, tahini, sea salt and vanilla extract. Give it a blast for a good 5 minutes, adding the measured boiling water gradually, until you have a nice smooth consistency. Pour into the cake tin on top of the base and stick it back into the freezer for at least 1 hour.

Corrr, we've come to the nicest part of this recipe, the indulgent caramel layer. Heat the coconut oil until liquid, add the maple syrup, almond butter and sea salt, and whisk into a smooth, sticky, gooey mixture. Get the cake tin from the freezer and cover the filling with the caramel. Back in the freezer again to firm up – 30 minutes max!

Right, we're capping it off now with a chocolate topping. Simply, warm the chocolate and coconut oil together until silky and shiny in a microwave or in a bowl over a pan of simmering water. Pour it over the caramel layer, give a final sprinkle of sea salt for decoration and stick it into the freezer for at least 2 hours to set.

When you're ready to have a bang on these, take it out of the freezer to defrost at least 2 hours before eating, then slice up. BOSH! Healthy, happy, win!

You'll need: traybake tin (pan)
33 x 23 x 5cm (13 x 9 x 2 inches)

Base
200g (1¹/₃ cups) pitted dried dates
200g (2 cups) walnuts
85g (3oz) raw/vegan chocolate
125g (¹/₂ cup) tahini (sesame) paste
5g (1 tbsp) cacao powder

Filling
800g (6²/₃ cups) cashew nuts
  (ideally soaked overnight)
100ml (scant ¹/₂ cup) coconut milk
100ml (scant ¹/₂ cup) maple syrup
150ml (scant ²/₃ cup) almond milk
75g (¹/₃ cup) tahini (sesame) paste
¹/₂ tsp sea salt
1 tsp vanilla extract
150ml (scant ²/₃ cup) boiling water

Caramel layer
210g (1 cup) coconut oil
315g (1 cup) maple syrup
175g (³/₄ cup) almond butter
1 tsp sea salt

Topping
340g (12oz) raw/vegan chocolate
50g (¹/₄ cup) coconut oil
1 tsp sea salt

Serves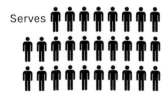

COCONUT & CHOCOLATE LAYER CAKE

We've taken one of our favourite combos – coconut and chocolate – and turned it into a vegan cake that tastes the bang bang and doesn't have so many of the naughty saturated fats you'll find in some of our other cakes.

Grease the cake tin (pan) and stick the kettle on. Soak the cashew nuts for the two layers in boiling water in individual bowls for at least an hour - preferably overnight. Soak your dates in boiling water for 10 minutes.

While the dates are soaking, whizz the walnuts to a chunky texture in a food processor. Strain the dates into a sieve and squeeze out the excess water. Throw the walnuts and dates into a bowl and mash them with your hands until the dates have broken down and the mixture binds together. Get the mix in the cake tin and, using the back of your fingers, push it evenly across the whole tin to make your base. Stick it in the freezer for 15 minutes to firm up.

For the filling, you need a food processor to get a smooth texture. Start with the coconut layer. Drain the cashews (making sure they're soft), then chuck them in the processor with the coconut milk, maple syrup and desiccated (shredded) coconut. Give it a blast for 5 minutes, gradually adding a small amount of hot water, until you have a smooth consistency. Pour into the cake tin, filling it halfway only. Place back in the freezer for 30 minutes to firm up quick!

It's exactly the same process for the chocolate layer but first melt the chocolate in the microwave (or heatproof bowl set over a pan of simmering water). Then, whizz up the soaked cashews along with the coconut milk, maple syrup and melted chocolate, adding some hot water to make a nice and smooth, velvety mix. In it goes on top of the coconut layer and then back in the freezer for at least 2 hours to set.

When you are ready to decorate, first make the chocolate drizzle. Melt the chocolate and coconut milk in the microwave (or heatproof bowl set over a pan of simmering water) for about 2 minutes, stirring every now and then. Drizzle it onto the cake, starting in the middle, using the back of a spoon to gently encourage the it over the edge. While the chocolate is still wet, sprinkle with the coconut pieces, coconut flakes, desiccated coconut and chocolate flakes. And there you go, you've just won at veganism!

Allow to defrost in the fridge for 3–4 hours before serving.

You'll need: 20cm (8 inch) deep springform cake tin (pan)

Base
350g (2 cups) pitted dried dates
225g (1²/₃ cups) walnuts

Coconut layer
200g (1²/₃ cups) cashew nuts (ideally soaked overnight)
200ml (generous ³/₄ cup) coconut milk
60ml (¹/₄ cup) maple syrup
40g (¹/₂ cup) desiccated (shredded) coconut

Chocolate layer
200g (1²/₃ cups) cashew nuts (ideally soaked overnight)
170g (6oz) dark chocolate (vegan)
200ml (generous ³/₄ cup) coconut milk
60ml (¹/₄ cup) maple syrup

Toppings
170g (6oz) dark chocolate (vegan)
150ml (scant ²/₃ cup) coconut milk
150g (5¹/₂oz) fresh coconut, broken into chunks
25g (¹/₂ cup) coconut flakes
25g (¹/₃ cup) desiccated (shredded) coconut
20g (³/₄oz) dark chocolate flakes (vegan)

Serves

AVOCADO & DARK CHOCOLATE MINIS

Avocado is such a versatile ingredient. It makes things double creamy and indulgent, but doesn't have the health risks of cream. This recipe is a proper banger with dark chocolate and can be enjoyed midweek or if you fancy a sweet treat but are watching those naughty calories. Quick! Simple! Tasty!

Stick the kettle on. You want to soak those cashew nuts in boiling water for at least an hour – preferably overnight. Then, soak your dates in boiling water for 10 minutes.

While the dates are soaking, whizz the walnuts and dark chocolate to a semi-coarse texture in a food processor. Strain the dates into a sieve and squeeze out any excess water. Throw the dates and walnuts into a bowl and mash and scrunch them with your hands, until the dates have broken down and the mixture all binds together. Divide evenly between the moulds, press down firmly with the back of your hand to make your base and place in the fridge for 15 minutes.

Drain the cashews (making sure they're soft), then chuck them into a food processor, along with the coconut milk, avocado and maple syrup. Give it a blast for a good 5–10 minutes to get a nice smooth consistency. While this is blending, melt the chocolate in the microwave for 2 minutes (or over a pan of simmering water).

Remove the cashews from the processor and stick into a bowl. Add the melted chocolate and semi-mix together to give a swirly effect. Pour into the moulds, level off with a palette knife and stick into the freezer for at least 2 hours to set.

For the topping, melt the dark chocolate and coconut oil in a microwave (or over a pan of simmering water) and pour onto each cake. Sprinkle with cacao nibs and a final zesting of lime.

Allow to defrost in the fridge for 1–2 hours before serving.

You'll need: 2 mini cheesecake moulds or a mini cheesecake tray (12 compartments)

Base
120g (³/₄ cup) pitted dried dates
40g (scant ¹/₂ cup) walnuts
10g (¹/₄oz) dark chocolate (vegan)

Filling
70g (generous ¹/₂ cup) cashew nuts (ideally soaked overnight)
50ml (scant ¹/₄ cup) coconut milk
140g (5oz) avocado flesh
30ml (2 tbsp) maple syrup
60g (2¹/₄oz) dark chocolate (vegan)

Topping
80g (2³/₄oz) dark chocolate (vegan)
10g (³/₄ tbsp) coconut oil
10g (4 tsp) cacao nibs
zest of ¹/₂ lime

Serves

COOKIES & CREAM SANDWICH

These are giant cookie sandwiches, with a biscuity base and a creamy cashew filling. We didn't want to end there – it didn't seem Pleesecakey enough – so we dipped them in chocolate to make them that bit more special! These can be made in batches and kept in the freezer to satisfy those sweet cravings!

Stick the kettle on. You want to soak those cashew nuts in boiling water for at least an hour – preferably overnight.

Whizz the biscuits to a fine crumb in a processor (stick 'em in a sandwich bag and bash with a rolling pin if you haven't got a processor). Add the melted coconut oil and give it a good stir to make sure that all the biscuit is nicely coated in butter. Place the rings on a baking tray and divide the biscuit mix evenly between them. Press down gently to make your base and place in the freezer for 15 minutes to firm up.

Drain the cashews (making sure they're soft), chuck them into a food processor along with the coconut milk, vanilla and maple syrup, and blast for 5–10 minutes, until smooth.

Pour the mixture into 10 of the rings (the other 10 rings contain the top cookies, so don't pour into those), leaving some space at the top of each ring for the other cookie to go on top. While the cashew mix is still wet, remove the 10 top cookies from the other rings and gently place them on top of the cashew mix on top of the bottom cookies to create the sandwich effect. Freeze for at least 2 hours to set.

When you are ready to decorate, finely scrape a few shavings from the dark chocolate – enough to sprinkle over your cookies. Then, melt the chocolate with the coconut oil for 1 minute in a microwave (or over a pan of simmering water). Remove the cookies from the freezer and take them out of the rings (a small blowtorch can help with this – just for a couple of seconds, or it'll start to melt). Dip half the cookie into the melted chocolate, remove and place onto some baking (parchment) paper. Repeat for all the cookies.

Working quickly so that the chocolate is still wet, blitz the Oreo biscuits to a fine crumb. Then, sprinkle the desiccated (shredded) coconut, biscuit crumb and choc shavings over the cookies. Stick 'em back in the freezer for 2 hours to set.

When you're ready to get stuck in, remove from the freezer and defrost in the fridge for 1–2 hours. These will keep in the freezer for up to a month, so you can always have a stash!

You'll need: 20 ring cutters 6cm (2½ inches) in diameter, 2.5cm (1 inch) tall

Base
300g (10½oz) Oreo biscuits
50g (¼ cup) coconut oil, melted

Filling
200g (1⅔ cups) cashew nuts (ideally soaked overnight)
150ml (scant ⅔ cup) coconut milk
2.5ml (½ tsp) vanilla extract
20ml (4 tsp) maple syrup

Topping
150g (5½oz) dark chocolate (vegan)
50g (¼ cup) coconut oil
20g (¾oz) Oreo biscuits
20g (¼ cup) desiccated (shredded) coconut

Serves

ALMOND & ORANGE CAKE

Have a bang on this one! Right, you're having pals round for dinner, you've got Camembert to start, followed by sticky ribs and chips. You still need a cap-off, but a sticky toffee pudding is going to send you over the edge. Holdtight, this almond and orange guilt-free number is the one! It's going to satisfy your sweet tooth for sure! Using blood orange segments in the topping adds a nice bit of contrast.

Grease the cake tin (pan) and stick the kettle on. You want to soak those cashew nuts in boiling water for at least an hour – preferably overnight. Then, soak your dates in boiling water for 10 minutes.

While the dates are soaking, whizz the almonds and macadamia nuts to a semi-coarse texture in a food processor. Strain the dates into a sieve and squeeze out any excess water. Throw the dates and nuts for the base into a bowl and mash and scrunch them with your hands, until the dates have broken down and the mixture all binds together.

Grab your cake tin and spread the base mixture evenly across the bottom with the back of your hand. Whack it in the freezer for 15 minutes while you crack on with the rest.

Drain the cashews (making sure they're soft), then chuck them into a food processor, along with the coconut milk, maple syrup, ground almonds, orange zest, and orange and almond extracts. Give it a blast for a good 5 minutes, until you have a nice smooth consistency. Pour the mixture into the cake tin, tap it on a hard surface to remove any air bubbles and level off with a palette knife. Stick it back in the freezer for at least 3 hours to set.

Once set, remove from the freezer and take it out of the tin. To decorate, lay the orange segments in a spiral pattern on top of the cake, starting from the outside and working inwards. To finish off, sprinkle with almond flakes and coconut sugar and orange zest. Done and dusted – there you have it, a decent-tasting vegan cake. Big up.

Allow to defrost in the fridge for 3–4 hours before serving.

You'll need: 20cm (8 inch) deep springform cake tin (pan)

Base
350g (2 cups) pitted dried dates
150g (generous 1 cup) almonds
75g (generous 3/4 cup) macadamia nuts

Filling
500g (4 1/4 cups) cashew nuts (ideally soaked overnight)
400ml (scant 1 2/3 cups) coconut milk
60ml (1/4 cup) maple syrup
50g (1/2 cup) ground almonds
zest of 1 large orange
20ml (4 tsp) orange extract
5ml (1 tsp) almond extract

Toppings
3 1/2 large oranges or blood oranges, segmented
20g (4 tbsp) flaked (sliced) almonds
zest of 1 orange
10g (1 tbsp) coconut sugar

Serves

CHOC ORANGE POPCORN

Anyone who's against or doesn't understand the vegan flex (which used to include both of us) needs to try this. Chocolate, orange and popcorn – undeniably incredible flavours that work so well together! If you're not a choc-orange fan, switch the orange for raspberry. Either way you're going to win with this one! Salivatingggg!

VEGAN

Grease the moulds and stick the kettle on. You want to soak those cashew nuts in boiling water for at least an hour - preferably overnight. Then, soak your dates in boiling water for 10 minutes.

Once the dates are nice and soft, strain them into a sieve and squeeze out any excess water. Throw them into a bowl with the popcorn and orange zest and mash and scrunch them with your hands, until the dates have broken down and the mixture all binds together. Divide evenly between the moulds, pressing down firmly with the back of your hand to form your bases. Whack them in the freezer for 15 minutes while you crack on with the rest.

Drain the cashews (making sure they're soft), then chuck them into a food processor with the coconut milk, orange extract and orange zest. Give it a blast for a good 5 minutes.

While this is blending, melt the dark chocolate in the microwave for 2 minutes (or over a pan of simmering water). Then, add the melted chocolate to the processor and blend further until it is a very smooth consistency. Stir through the popcorn until evenly distributed. Spoon into the moulds and stick in the freezer for at least 2 hours to set.

Once set, remove from the freezer and take them out of the moulds (a small blowtorch can help with this - just for a couple of seconds, or it'll start to melt). Melt the dark chocolate and coconut oil in the microwave for 1 minute (or over a pan of simmering water). Spread an even layer of chocolate over the tops of the cakes to create a sticky foundation. Then, add a layer of popcorn while the chocolate is still wet. Drizzle with more melted chocolate, followed by more popcorn. Repeat the process until you have a popcorn tower stuck together with chocolate. A final drizzle of chocolate and a grating of orange zest is all that's needed to finish off these proper tasty vegan cakes!

Allow to defrost in the fridge for 1–2 hours before serving.

You'll need: 2 mini cheesecake moulds or a mini cheesecake tray (12 compartments)

Base
120g (¾ cup) pitted dried dates
5g (1 cup) popcorn
zest of 1 orange

Filling
75g (⅔ cup) cashew nuts (ideally soaked overnight)
55ml (scant ¼ cup) coconut milk
5ml (1 tsp) orange extract
zest of ½ orange
60g (2¼oz) dark chocolate (vegan)
20g (3½ cups) popcorn

Topping
60g (2¼oz) dark chocolate (vegan)
10g (¾ tbsp) coconut oil
25g (3½ cups) popcorn
zest of ½ orange

Serves

GUILT-FREE SUMMER FRUIT PLEESECAKE

Simple yet effective, this summer fruit vegan cake is quality and guilt free. Vegan or not vegan, you'll love this any day of the week, to refresh on a hot summer's day or as a pick-me-up on a moody rainy day.

Grease the cake tin (pan) and stick the kettle on. You want to soak those cashew nuts in boiling water for at least an hour – preferably overnight. Then, soak your dates in boiling water for 10 minutes.

While the dates are soaking, whizz the walnuts to a semi-coarse texture in a food processor. Strain the dates into a sieve and squeeze out any excess water. Throw the dates and walnuts into a bowl and mash and scrunch them with your hands, until the dates have broken down and the mixture all binds together. Grab your cake tin and spread the base mixture evenly across the bottom with the back of your hand. Whack it in the freezer for 20 minutes while you crack on with the rest.

For the filling, drain the cashew nuts (making sure they're soft), then chuck them into the food processor along with the coconut milk, maple syrup and the frozen summer berries. Give it a blast for a good 5 minutes, until you have a nice smooth, lump-free consistency. Pour the mixture into the cake tin, tap it on a hard surface to remove any air bubbles and level off with a palette knife. Stick it back in the freezer for at least 3 hours to set.

Once set, remove from the freezer and take it out of the tin.

To make it look pretty, cut up and arrange the summer fruits all over the surface. A drizzle of compote and some fresh mint, and there you have it – another vegan cake that's going to impress!

Allow to defrost in the fridge for 3–4 hours before serving.

You'll need: 20cm (8 inch) deep springform cake tin (pan)

Base
350g (2 cups) pitted dried dates
225g (1²/₃ cups) walnuts

Filling
500g (4¹/₄ cups) cashew nuts (ideally soaked overnight)
400ml (scant 1²/₃ cups) coconut milk
60ml (¹/₄ cup) maple syrup
225g (8oz) frozen summer berries

Topping
400g (14oz) mixed fruits
350g (12oz) berry compote
a few mint leaves

Serves

LEMON & RASPBERRY MINIS

These banging little fresh Kev Keegan (vegan) minis are lovely. Proper tasty little puds to be enjoyed if you want an alternative to a full-on guilty choice and you've just had a mad blow-out weekend but still need that sweet fix. We ain't about making boring vegan cakes, we're here to make things taste GREAT, so if you like your food you'll love these!

Right we're about ... get your kettle on. You want to soak those cashew nuts in boiling water for at least an hour – preferably overnight. Then, soak your dates in boiling water for 10 minutes.

While the dates are soaking, whizz the walnuts to a semi-coarse texture in a food processor. Strain the dates into a sieve and squeeze out any excess water. Throw the dates and walnuts into a bowl, and mash and scrunch them with your hands, until the dates have broken down and the mixture all binds together. Divide evenly into four balls and press each one firmly into the moulds with the back of your hand. Whack in the freezer for 15 minutes to firm up.

Drain the cashews (making sure they're soft), then chuck them into a food processor, along with the coconut milk, maple syrup, lemon juice and zest, and half the raspberries. Give it a blast for a good 5 minutes, until you have a nice smooth consistency with no lumps.

Get your bases out of the freezer and whack in the remaining raspberries around the edge of the moulds, flat (top) side down, to form a raspberry wall. Then spoon in your filling, level off with a palette knife and whack back in the freezer for at least 2 hours to set.

Once set, remove from the freezer and take them out of the moulds.

For the coulis, simply blend the raspberries and maple syrup in a food processor. To top, first spoon on some coulis followed by the raspberries (about 7 raspberries per cake). And there you have it, a banging little vegan cake.

Allow to defrost in the fridge for 1–2 hours before serving.

You'll need: 4 mini cheesecake moulds or a mini cheesecake tray (12 compartments)

Base
280g (1²/₃ cups) pitted dried dates
70g (¹/₂ cup) walnuts

Filling
145g (1¹/₄ cups) cashew nuts (ideally soaked overnight)
115ml (scant ¹/₂ cup) coconut milk
60ml (¹/₄ cup) maple syrup
juice of 4 lemons
zest of 2 lemons
180g (1¹/₃ cups) raspberries

Raspberry coulis
60g (¹/₂ cup) raspberries
10ml (2 tsp) maple syrup

Topping
35g (¹/₄ cup) raspberries
zest of 1 lemon

Serves

FULLY LOADED

STRAWBERRY EDGE LEDGE

THE BC CAKE

STRAWBERRY & LEMON LAYER CAKE

Shirls

COR

Classic Pleesecakes

FULLY DIPPED
RRRRRRRS

STRAWBERRY EDGE LEDGE

This was one of the first ever cheesecakes we made, even before Pleesecakes was formed. It's been around for the entirety of Pleesecakes and sits proudly in our classics section. Being such a showstopper, it's a regular request for wedding cakes! We've kept it very simple and it can easily be adapted to flavours or ingredients that you prefer or think would work better. There's no right or wrong with this one and a chocolate filling would work a dream too! You've gotta make this recipe – it's great for photos and guaranteed to get you a few likes on Insta!

Whizz the digestive biscuits to a fine crumb in a food processor (stick 'em in a sandwich bag and bash with a rolling pin if you haven't got a processor). Add the melted butter and give it a good stir to make sure that all the biscuit is nicely coated. Pour into the cake tin (pan) and press down gently and evenly to make your base. Level off around the edge with the back of a spoon and place in the freezer for 15 minutes to firm up.

To make the filling, beat the cream cheese and 100g (½ cup) sugar together. Blitz the strawberries in a food processor with the remaining sugar to a purée. Then, add the strawberry purée to the cream cheese and mix together thoroughly. Whip the cream until you have stiff peaks and fold it gently into the mix. Put to one side.

For the strawberry edge, cut the green ends off the strawberries and slice in half lengthways. Grab the cake tin and stick the strawberries around the edge (with the flat inside edge of the strawberry facing outwards). Spoon in the cheese mixture, starting gently around the edge with small spoonfuls, making sure you don't dislodge the strawberries, and working your way into the middle. Level off with a palette knife and then run your forefinger and thumb around the rim of the tin to create a professional finish. Tap the tin gently on a hard surface to remove any air bubbles. Stick it in the fridge for at least 4 hours to set.

Once set, remove from the freezer and take it out of the cake tin. Top first with the mixed berry compote, then the fresh fruit. This one's ready to serve straight away.

You'll need: 23cm (9 inch) deep
 springform cake tin (pan)

Base
440g (15½oz) plain digestive biscuits
**50g (3½ tbsp) unsalted butter,
 melted**

Filling
920g (2lb) cream cheese
**125g (⅔ cup) caster (superfine)
 sugar**
100g (1 cup) strawberries
**300ml (1¼ cups) double (heavy)
 cream**

Edge
190g (scant 2 cups) strawberries

Topping
300g (10½oz) mixed berry compote
100g (1 cup) strawberries
100g (¾ cup) blueberries
100g (¾ cup) raspberries
75g (½ cup) blackberries

Serves

Get tagging us on Insta with your
version of this cake using the hashtag
#bcpleesecake

THE BC CAKE

We originally made this beast for our good pal the BC (Body Coach). He's been a top boy since the beginning of Pleesecakes, giving us a shout-out on Insta in Jan 2017, getting the business off the ground. It seemed only fair to name a Pleesecake after him. Nice one Wicksy, here's to cheesecake and HIITS!

Whizz the biscuits to a fine crumb in a food processor (or stick 'em in a sandwich bag and bash with a rolling pin). Add the melted butter, give it a good stir to make sure that all the biscuit is nicely coated, then mix in the choc drops. Pour into the cake tin (pan) and press down gently and evenly to make your base. Level off around the edge with the back of a spoon and place in the freezer for 15 minutes to firm up.

Beat the cream cheese and sugar together. Add the chocolate hazelnut spread and mix together thoroughly. Whip the cream until you have stiff peaks and fold it gently into the mix.

This next bit's slightly tricky. Cut the Ferrero Rocher in half – a sharp knife is the key. Press the halves around the edge of the cake tin (with the flat inside edge facing outwards). Packing them in tight, being careful not to crush them, is the way to get them to stay standing up.

Spoon in the cheese mixture, starting gently around the edge with small spoonfuls, making sure you don't dislodge the Ferrero Rocher, and working your way into the middle. Level off with a palette knife and then run your forefinger and thumb around the rim of the tin to create a professional finish! Tap the tin gently on a hard surface to remove any air bubbles. Stick it in the freezer for at least 2 hours to set.

Topping time! Remove the cake from the tin and secure it on a cake board using some hazelnut spread. To make the chocolate drizzle, blitz the dark and milk chocolate into a coarse crumb and whack it in a heatproof bowl. Heat the cream until piping hot (but not bubbling)! Pour the cream onto the chocolate gradually, stirring as you go, making sure the consistency is not too thick or too thin. Then drizzle it onto the cake, starting in the middle and using the back of a spoon to gently encourage the chocolate over the edge.

While the chocolate is still wet, start adding the toppings to secure everything in place. Remember, there's no right or wrong with this! When you're done creating, allow to defrost in the fridge for 3–4 hours before serving.

You'll need: 20cm (8 inch) deep springform cake tin (pan)

Base
360g (12³/₄oz) double chocolate digestive biscuits
30g (2 tbsp) unsalted butter, melted
15g (¹/₂oz) dark chocolate drops
15g (¹/₂oz) milk chocolate drops

Filling
720g (1lb 9oz) cream cheese
80g (generous ¹/₃ cup) caster (superfine) sugar
400g (1¹/₃ cups) chocolate hazelnut spread
200ml (generous ³/₄ cup) double (heavy) cream

Edge
10¹/₂ Ferrero Rocher hazelnut chocolate balls

Topping
100g (3¹/₂oz) dark chocolate
100g (3¹/₂oz) milk chocolate
150ml (scant ²/₃ cup) double (heavy) cream
a big pile of choccy treats

Serves

If you don't know what you're doing, don't worry, just

MAKE IT UP AS YOU GO ALONG AND KEEP ON GOING!

Step outside the box and be fearless. Chucking yourself in at the deep end is key, you either win or learn, you'll never lose! Adapt to each situation, learn from it and win!

Two painters turned cheesecake entrepreneurs **anything is possible!**

FULLY LOADED

The Fully Loaded Pleesecake was conceived within one week of opening and it's one of our classics! We were all over the place, still finding our feet in the cake industry having just swapped over from the painting and decorating world, experimenting with toppings and flavours and trying to create a cake that was going to have the wow factor. The filling is mostly caramel, which is one of our favourite flavours, so we just had to smash it in and get it on a cheesecake! Pure unadulterated filth!

Whizz the biscuits to a fine crumb in a food processor (stick 'em in a sandwich bag and bash with a rolling pin if you haven't got a processor) and whack them in a mixing bowl. Add the melted butter and give it a good stir to make sure that all the biscuit is nicely coated, then mix in the mini fudge, dark choc drops and popcorn. Pour into the cake tin (pan) and press down gently and evenly to make your base. Level off around the edge with the back of a spoon and place in the freezer for 15 minutes to firm up.

Beat the cream cheese and sugar together. Add the salted caramel sauce, sea salt, and mini fudge pieces, and mix together thoroughly. Whip the cream until you have stiff peaks and fold it gently into the mix. Spoon into the cake tin, level off with a palette knife, then run your forefinger and thumb around the rim of the tin to create a professional finish. Tap the tin gently on a hard surface to remove any air bubbles. Stick it into the freezer for at least 3 hours to set.

When you're ready, get building a fully loaded beaut! Our tip is to start with the big bulky things to create a good foundation. Then move onto the slightly smaller bars and work your way down in size until you get to the little things for the finishing touches. But there's no correct way of constructing this cake. So, we're setting you another challenge, the fully loaded challenge! We want to see your fully loaded creations! Let's get creative and get tagging #fullyloadedchallenge.

Allow to defrost in the fridge for 3–4 hours before serving.

You'll need: 23cm (9 inch) deep springform cake tin (pan)

Base
420g (15oz) double chocolate digestive biscuits
60g (¼ cup) unsalted butter, melted
20g (³/₄oz) mini fudge pieces
20g (³/₄oz) dark chocolate drops
20g (³/₄oz) toffee popcorn

Filling
990g (2lb 3oz) cream cheese
110g (generous ½ cup) caster (superfine) sugar
415g (1¼ cups) salted caramel sauce
1 tsp sea salt
35g (1¼oz) mini fudge pieces
250ml (1 cup) double (heavy) cream

Topping
500–700g (1lb 2oz–1lb 9oz) of your favourite chocolate and wafers in varying sizes and shapes – get creative!

Serves

CORRRRRRRRS

You know the story, we downed tools, walked off-site and decided to enter the dessert industry. Bear in mind, neither of us had ever spent a day in a commercial kitchen, let alone had any sort of training or catering qualification under our belts. Go forth into the darkness … Even so, we ended up creating these pretty unique cheesecakes. But, we didn't settle at that – we know we have to keep learning and improving what we do. One day, we stumbled across pots of ice cream with a caramel core, accidentally buying them maybe twice, three times a week. It's a bit annoying when that happens. But hey, the Core Pleesecake was born and it was something we were excited to share, cos who don't love a decent cheesecake with a massive caramel core??? That's right, no one!

Core skills

Use a plastic water bottle (or similar) to create this Pleesecake's unique caramel core. The bottle needs to have smooth, straight sides in order for this to work. Don't use one with ridged sides.

1. Once you've got your base into your tin, and it's nicely firmed up, place the empty bottle into the middle of the tin.

2. Pour your filling carefully around the bottle, making sure the bottle stays roughly in the centre of the tin.

3. Freeze the cake, allowing it to set with the bottle in place. To remove the bottle, you can pour in a little hot water to help it slide out.

See the next page for the full recipe.

Whizz the biscuits to a fine crumb in a food processor (stick 'em in a sandwich bag and bash with a rolling pin if you haven't got a processor). Add the melted butter and give it a good stir to make sure that all the biscuit is nicely coated, then mix in the chocolate buttons and malt balls. Pour into the cake tin (pan) and press down gently and evenly to make your base. Level off around the edge with the back of a spoon and place in the freezer for 15 minutes to firm up.

Beat the cream cheese and sugar together. Add the chocolate spread and mix together thoroughly. Whip the cream until you have stiff peaks and fold it gently into the mix.

Before you transfer the filling into the cake tin, you want to get that plastic bottle in the centre (see page 68), then spoon the filling mix in around it. Level off with a palette knife and then run your forefinger and thumb around the rim of the tin to create a professional finish. Tap the tin gently on a hard surface to remove any air bubbles. Stick it in the freezer for at least 3 hours to set.

Once frozen, remove from the freezer and release the springform sides, keeping the base in place. Pour hot water into the plastic bottle to make it easier to slide it out. Spoon that double-naughty caramel sauce into the inviting hole and fill to the top.

To make the chocolate drizzle, blitz the milk and dark chocolate into a coarse crumb and whack it in a heatproof bowl. Heat the cream until piping hot (but not bubbling). Pour the cream onto the chocolate gradually, stirring as you go, making sure the consistency is not too thick or too thin. Then drizzle it onto the cake, starting in the middle and using the back of a spoon to gently encourage the chocolate over the edge. Try not to cover the core.

To decorate, arrange all your favourite sweets, chocolate or fruits in a ring around the core. What you're creating is a cheesecake fondue, so all the decoration can be used to dip into the core! CORRRRRRRR, how good does that sound?!!! Guaranteed you'll be giving that a go now!

Allow to defrost in the fridge for 3–4 hours before serving.

You'll need: 23cm (9 inch) deep springform cake tin (pan); 7.5cm (3-inch) plastic bottle (see page 68)

Base
440g (15¹/₂oz) plain digestive biscuits
90g (generous ¹/₃ cup) unsalted butter, melted
60g (2¹/₄oz) milk chocolate buttons
70g (2¹/₂oz) chocolate malt balls

Filling
810g (1lb 12oz cups) cream cheese
90g (scant ¹/₂ cup) caster (superfine) sugar
300g (1 cup) chocolate spread
200ml (generous ³/₄ cup) double (heavy) cream

Core
230g (²/₃ cup) caramel sauce

Topping
125g (4¹/₂oz) milk chocolate
125g (4¹/₂oz) dark chocolate
185ml (³/₄ cup) double (heavy) cream
500–600g (1lb 2oz–1lb 5oz) fruits/ sweets/chocolate

Serves

STRAWBERRY & LEMON LAYER CAKE

We've given you this flavour combo because we think it's a winner, but you can literally use whatever your favourite guilty pleasures are. Peanut butter and chocolate hazelnut, vanilla and chocolate, passionfruit and raspberry ... there are endless options out there!!

Whizz the biscuits to a fine crumb in a food processor (stick 'em in a sandwich bag and bash with a rolling pin if you haven't got a processor). Add the melted butter and give it a good stir to make sure that all the biscuit is nicely coated, then mix in the freeze-dried strawberries and the lemon zest. Pour into the cake tin and press down gently and evenly to make your base. Level off around the edge with the back of a spoon and place into the freezer for 15 minutes to firm up.

For the lemon layer, beat the cream cheese and sugar together. Add the lemon juice and lemon essence, and mix together thoroughly. Whip the cream until you have stiff peaks and fold it gently into the mix. Spoon into the cake tin and level off with a spatula, then neaten the edge with some kitchen roll. Stick it in the freezer for 45 minutes to set.

Meanwhile, make the strawberry layer in the same way, but first blitzing the strawberries with 2½ tsp sugar in a food processor to make a purée. Then, beat the cream cheese and remaining sugar together, mix through the strawberry purée and finally fold in the whipped cream.

When the lemon layer is slightly set, pour the strawberry layer on top and level off with a palette knife. Stick it back into the freezer for at least 2 hours to set.

Once firm, remove from the freezer, take it out of the mould and simply top with some mixed fresh fruit. Before serving, allow to defrost in the fridge for 3-4 hours.

You'll need: 20cm (8 inch) deep springform cake tin (pan)

Base
360g (12¾oz) plain digestive biscuits
100g (scant ½ cup) unsalted butter, melted
3 tbsp freeze-dried strawberries
zest of 1 lemon

Lemon layer
430g (15oz) cream cheese
70g (⅓ cup) caster (superfine) sugar
30ml (2 tbsp) lemon juice
5ml (1 tsp) lemon essence
75ml (scant ⅓ cup) double (heavy) cream

Strawberry layer
40g (scant ½ cup) strawberries
60g (⅓ cup) caster (superfine) sugar
430g (15oz) cream cheese
75ml (scant ⅓ cup) double (heavy) cream

Topping
400–500g (14oz–1lb 2oz) mixed fresh fruit

Serves 🧍🧍🧍🧍🧍🧍🧍 - 🧍🧍

SWIRLS

The swirl cake is for people who cannot be bothered with accuracy and want to make a quick and easy dessert that's going to look MUCH more impressive compared with the amount of actual work that went into it! It's really adaptable, so you can use almost anything you've got lying around in your cupboards. This one's a bowl licker too, so get the whole family involved!

Whizz both the biscuits to a fine crumb in a food processor (stick 'em in a sandwich bag and bash with a rolling pin if you haven't got a processor). Add the melted butter, and give it a good stir to make sure that all the biscuit is nicely coated . Pour into the cake tin (pan) and press down gently and evenly to make your base. Level off around the edge with the back of a spoon and place in the freezer for 15 minutes to firm up.

Beat the cream cheese and sugar together. Add the vanilla paste and mix together thoroughly. Whip the cream until you have stiff peaks and fold it gently into the mix. Melt the dark and milk chocolate in the microwave or in a heatproof bowl set over a pan of simmering water. Pour the melted chocolate into the cheese mixture and semi-mix it in to create the swirl effect. Spoon into the cake tin and level off with a palette knife. Stick it in the freezer for at least 3 hours to set.

Remove from the freezer and take it out of the tin – now it's time to conjure up your creative side. We are going to set you a challenge to create the most spectacular cake! Tag us in your creations on Insta using the hashtag #swirlpleesecakechallenge. We can't wait to see what you come up with!

Allow to defrost in the fridge for 3–4 hours before serving.

You'll need: 20cm (8 inch) deep springform cake tin (pan)

Base
180g (6¼oz) double chocolate digestive biscuits
180g (6¼oz) plain digestive biscuits
45g (3 tbsp) unsalted butter, melted

Filling
920g (2lb) cream cheese
85g (scant ½ cup) caster (superfine) sugar
60g (4 tbsp) vanilla bean paste
200ml (generous ¾ cup) double (heavy) cream
100g (3½oz) dark chocolate
100g (3½oz) milk chocolate

Topping
600–800g (1lb 5oz–1lb 12oz) fruits/ sweets/chocolate/confectionery (there's no right or wrong – get creative! Take a look at our Instagram page for some inspiration #cakeinspo)

Serves 👤👤👤👤👤👤👤👤 - 👤👤

FULLY DIPPED

Another one of our crazy ideas. We've dipped the whole cheesecake in chocolate and added dangerously sharp chocolate shards coming out of it! This one's a head turner and a sure talking point at any party.

Whizz the biscuits to a fine crumb in a food processor (stick 'em in a sandwich bag and bash with a rolling pin if you haven't got a processor). Add the melted butter and give it a good stir to make sure that all the biscuit is nicely coated, then mix in the mini fudge pieces and choc drops. Divide evenly between the moulds, press down gently to make your bases and place in the freezer for 15 minutes to firm up.

Beat the cream cheese and sugar together. Blitz the Oreo biscuits to a fine crumb in the food processor, and add them to the cream cheese, along with the chocolate spread, and mix together thoroughly. Whip the cream until you have stiff peaks and fold it gently into the mix. Spoon into the moulds and level off with a palette knife. Stick 'em back in the freezer for at least 2 hours to set.

Meanwhile, make the chocolate shards. Line a baking sheet with baking (parchment) paper. Melt the dark and white chocolate separately in the microwave or in heatproof bowls set over a pan of simmering water, then spread out all over the baking sheet, swirling them together (roughly 2mm/ 1/8 inch thick). Whack it in the freezer for 30 minutes to set.

When the cakes are set, remove from the freezer and take out of the moulds, and we're ready to dip these beauts. To make the chocolate coating, blitz the dark chocolate into a coarse crumb in the food processor and whack it in a heatproof bowl. Heat the cream until piping hot (but not bubbling). Pour the cream onto the chocolate gradually, stirring as you go, making sure the consistency is smooth and lump-free. Allow the coating to cool slightly, but not set.

Dip the cakes in the chocolate sauce, submerging almost all the way to base, and place on a rack ready to decorate.

Working fast, while the chocolate coating is still wet, remove the chocolate from the freezer and break into shards. Jab the shards and the large chocolate buttons into the cakes. Blitz the Oreo biscuits to a fine crumb and sprinkle over the top. Add a final sprinkling of choc drops and stick it back in the freezer for 30 minutes to set.

Allow to defrost in the fridge for 1–2 hours before serving.

You'll need: 4 mini cheesecake moulds or a mini cheesecake tray (12 compartments)

Base
120g (4¼oz) plain digestive biscuits
40g (3 tbsp) unsalted butter, melted
20g (¾oz) mini fudge pieces
20g (¾oz) milk chocolate drops

Filling
360g (12¾oz) cream cheese
60g (⅓ cup) caster (superfine) sugar
60g (2¼oz) Oreo biscuits
140g (½ cup) chocolate spread
140ml (scant ⅔ cup) double (heavy) cream

Chocolate shards
100g (3½oz) dark chocolate
100g (3½oz) white chocolate

Coating
300g (10½oz) dark chocolate
180ml (¾ cup) double (heavy) cream

Topping
20g (¾oz) Oreo biscuits
10g (¼oz) milk chocolate drops
10g (¼oz) dark chocolate drops
16 large chocolate buttons

Serves 🙌🙌🙌🙌

PEANUT BUTTER & MARMITE MINIS

melon & parma ham cups

SWEET DREAMS ARE MADE OF BRIE & CRANBERRY

WINGIN' IT

MAC &

salmon & herb bites

CHEESECAKE

BEETROOT & FETA MINIS

cheeseboard cheesecake

RUBY MURRAY MINIS

CHORIZO & ROASTED RED PEPPER BITES

CHEESEBOARD CHEESECAKE

This one's for the proper cheese fans. Obviously, cheese is life, and we've really gone to town on this one. It's been a popular seller for us over the last year, just because it's so different. It's entirely adaptable to your cheeses of choice, but this is based on what we like. A nice variety of cheeses at the end of a double indulgent meal hits the spot every time. This one's a centrepiece sharer, so you can openly advertise to your pals and family that you've got a cheeseboard cheesecake for dessert and see them all come running!

Whizz the crackers into a coarse crumb in a food processor (stick 'em in a sandwich bag and bash with a rolling pin if you haven't got a processor). Add the melted butter and give it a good stir to make sure that all the crackers are nicely coated. Pour into the cake tin (pan) and press down gently and evenly to make your base. Level off around the edge with the back of a spoon and place in the fridge for 30 minutes to firm up.

For the filling, it's as simple as mixing the cream cheese, chutney and a pinch of salt and pepper together. Spoon onto the cracker base and level off with a palette knife. Stick it back in the fridge for at least 2 hours to set.

Once set, remove from the fridge and take it out of the tin. Time to get creative. Get your favourite cheeses, cut and break them into different shapes and sizes, and place on top of the cake using the caramelized onion chutney to hold things in place. Slot the figs, celery, gherkins, grapes and pickled onions in between all the gaps. Add the sprigs of redcurrants and rosemary and sprinkle over the thyme leaves for a proper decent-looking cheeseboard cheesecake. Put this in the centre of a table and you're guaranteed to have some happy faces!

Serves 👤👤👤👤👤👤👤👤👤👤👤 - 🏃🏃

You'll need: 20cm (8 inch) deep springform cake tin (pan)

Base
250g (9oz) cream (savoury) crackers
160g (scant ¾ cup) butter, melted

Filling
920g (2lb) cream cheese
150g (½ cup) apple and pear spiced chutney
salt and pepper

Topping
200g (7oz) Stilton cheese
125g (4½oz) mature Cheddar cheese
125g (4½oz) red Leicester cheese
80g (2¾oz) Brie
300g (1 cup) caramelized onion chutney
3 figs
2 or 3 celery sticks
100g (3½oz) mini gherkins
150g (5½oz) seedless grapes
50g (1¾oz) mini pickled onions
a few sprigs of redcurrants
2 fresh rosemary sprigs
leaves from 1 fresh thyme sprig

MAC & CHEESECAKE

This was a bit of a lightbulb moment for us! Macaroni cheese? Yes please. Cheesecake? Sure! How can we turn this into something magical, combining two of our great loves into one dish? Do not worry, people, for we have come up with a right old corker. This one's part of our savoury selection, because you can't have a sweet without some savoury beforehand, can you?! Dun, Dun, Dun... we give you the MAC & CHEESECAKE ... AARRRRRRRR!

Holdtight, let's go! Preheat the oven to 200°C (400°F/gas mark 6). Stick the kettle on and boil some water for the pasta. Get your pasta in as soon as it's boiling, and cook for 8–10 minutes until tender. We want to move quick on this one – it tastes too good to wait around!

To make the base for this magical filling, start off by frying the onion and the pancetta for 5–6 minutes until the pancetta is crisp. Add the Parmesan and the breadcrumbs and fry for a further 2 minutes. Press the breadcrumb mix into the dishes.

Drain the pasta and chuck it in a bowl. Add the Parmesan, Cheddar, Stilton (if using) and cream cheese. Throw in some dried thyme and a pinch of salt and pepper, and give it a proper toss!

Lovingly pour the pasta mix onto the crispy breadcrumb base – don't be afraid of some spillage, it's all part of the experience! Whack on the topping cream cheese and Cheddar, sprinkle with a few more breadcrumbs and stick it in the oven for 20–25 minutes to become pure heaven!

Once golden and gooey, take it out of the oven, sprinkle with fresh thyme and you're ready to serve up. THAT'S A BIG WIN THERE!

You'll need: 2 small baking dishes

Base
1 onion, finely chopped
150g (5¹/₂oz) pancetta, cubed
50g (²/₃ cup) freshly grated
   Parmesan cheese
70g (1¹/₂ cups) fresh breadcrumbs

Filling
100g (3¹/₂oz) tagliatelle
100g (3¹/₂oz) rigatoni
50g (²/₃ cup) freshly grated
   Parmesan cheese
250g (9oz) Cheddar cheese, grated
50g (1³/₄oz) Stilton cheese,
   crumbled (optional)
120g (¹/₂ cup) cream cheese
¹/₄ tsp dried thyme
salt and pepper

Topping
20g (1¹/₂ tbsp) cream cheese
20g (³/₄oz) Cheddar cheese, grated
10g (¹/₄ cup) fresh breadcrumbs
leaves from 2 fresh thyme sprigs

Serves

CHORIZO & ROASTED RED PEPPER BITES

Being proper foodies, we love going to new places, here and abroad, to try new flavours and foods. One ingredient always making regular appearances is the famous Spanish sausage – chorizo! Being such big fans, we had no choice but to incorporate that heavenly little sausage into one of our Pleesecake creations.

Preheat your oven to 200°C (400°F/gas mark 6). In a large bowl, smash up the tortilla chips. Mix through the grated (shredded) Cheddar. Divide the cheesy mix evenly into 12 portions, stick it in 12 moulds and press down gently to make your base. Whack them in the oven for 8 minutes until the cheese softens and holds the mix together.

Chop the topping chorizo into 12 thin slices, put them on a baking sheet and get them in the oven for about 7 minutes.

Put a frying pan over a medium heat and fry off the filling chorizo, roasted pepper, garlic and spring onion (scallion) for 5 minutes, then set aside to cool.

By the time you've done that, your bases and chorizo crisps will be done, so get them out and leave to one side to cool.

When everything is cooled down, put the cream cheese in a bowl with the red pepper and chorizo mix, season with salt and pepper and chilli flakes (crushed chili pepper) and give it a good stir. Spoon the mix into the moulds on top of the tortilla base. Stick 'em in the fridge for 30–45 minutes to set.

While you're waiting, the consumption of a glass of Rioja is recommended, but entirely optional.

Time's up, get them bitesized beauties out the fridge!

Gently pop them out of the moulds and get them on a fancy serving board, to impress any Tom, Dick or Harry who walks through the front door! Decorate each one with the chorizo crisps you made earlier, sprinkle with chilli flakes and give them all a squeeze of lime, then chuck on the spring onions. Stick some more tortillas on the board to help scoop up any fallen stray bits of chorizo. Now get stuck in. Personally, we think a few jalapeños go down an absolute treat with these!

You'll need: bitesize mini cheesecake tray (20 compartments)

Base
180g (6¹/₄oz) chilli flavour tortilla chips
200g (7oz) Cheddar cheese, grated

Filling
120g (4¹/₄ oz) chorizo, finely chopped
1 roasted red pepper (the ones from a jar are great), finely chopped
1 garlic clove, finely chopped
1 spring onion (scallion), finely chopped
720g (1lb 9oz) cream cheese
1 tsp chilli flakes (crushed chili pepper)
salt and pepper

Topping
30g (1oz) chorizo
chilli flakes (crushed chili pepper)
1 lime
2 spring onions (scallions), thinly sliced
20g (³/₄oz) jalapeños
handful of tortilla chips

Serves

PEANUT BUTTER & MARMITE MINIS

If you haven't tried creamy peanut butter and salty Marmite on toast, do so immediately! We ain't trying to be clever or different with these recipes, we're just translating some of our favourite food combinations into cheesecakes! We eat these foods, we know they work well together – and they're even better as a Pleesecake!

Whizz the digestive biscuits and half the peanuts to a fine crumb in a food processor. Add the melted butter, and give it a good stir to make sure that everything is nicely coated, then mix in the remaining peanuts. Divide evenly between the moulds, press down gently to make your base and place in the fridge for 30 minutes to firm up.

For the filling, beat the cream cheese and the sugar together. Add the peanut butter and Marmite, and mix together thoroughly. Whip the cream until you have stiff peaks and fold it gently into the mix. Spoon into moulds and level off with a palette knife. Whack 'em back in the fridge for at least 2 hours to set.

For the nut brittle, line a baking sheet with baking (parchment) paper. Melt the sugar in a saucepan until silky and golden brown, then remove from the heat. Stir in the nuts, making sure they are all coated in sugar, and pour onto the baking sheet. Let it cool for an hour.

Once the brittle is cooled and the filling is set, remove the cheesecakes from the fridge and take them out of the moulds. Break up the brittle and place a healthy chunk on each cake. To finish, drizzle with Marmite and serve! Different, yet tasty!!!

You'll need: 3 mini cheesecake moulds or a mini cheesecake tray (12 compartments)

Base
115g (4oz) plain digestive biscuits
55g (generous 1/3 cup) peanuts
30g (2 tbsp) unsalted butter, melted

Filling
230g (1 cup) cream cheese
30g (2¹/₂ tbsp) caster (superfine) sugar
70g (¹/₃ cup) peanut butter
45g (2¹/₂ tbsp) Marmite or other yeast extract
140ml (scant ²/₃ cup) double (heavy) cream

Peanut and cashew brittle
150g (³/₄ cup) caster (superfine) sugar
75g (scant ¹/₂ cup) peanuts
75g (generous ¹/₂ cup) cashew nuts

Topping
10g (¹/₂ tbsp) Marmite or other yeast extract

Serves 👤👤👤

SALMON & HERB BITES

This classic flavour combo has always been around, so we put our Pleesecake stamp on it and turned it into a quick and easy recipe for proper tasty bitesized pieces of heaven. Great for a starter or canapé!

Preheat the oven to 180°C (350°F/gas mark 4). For the base, cut the ciabatta into 12 small discs using the ring cutter. Rub the discs with the garlic and drizzle with olive oil. Place on a baking sheet and put into the oven for about 5 minutes or until lightly toasted. Set aside to cool.

For the filling, add the finely chopped herbs and garlic to the cream cheese and mix together thoroughly. Next, add the lemon juice, along with a pinch of salt and pepper, and set to one side.

For the herb drizzle, whack the mixed herbs, garlic and olive oil in a pestle and mortar, and grind to a paste. Adjust accordingly, adding olive oil to make it looser if required.

Next, spoon the cheese mixture onto the cooled ciabatta rings.

Drape the smoked salmon over the top, drizzle with that herb dressing, garnish with the chives and they're ready to serve!

You'll need: 5cm (2 inch) ring cutter

Base
1 loaf ciabatta bread
1 garlic clove
olive oil

Filling
**handful of flat-leaf parsley,
  finely chopped**
25g (³/₄oz) chives, finely chopped
2 garlic cloves, finely chopped
720g (1lb 9oz) cream cheese
juice of 1 lemon
salt and pepper

Herb drizzle
15g (¹/₂oz) chives
15g (¹/₂oz) parsley
1 garlic clove, finely chopped
**30ml (2 tbsp) olive oil, plus extra
  if needed**

Topping
**120g (4¹/₄oz) smoked salmon, cut into
  small strips**
few chives, snipped into long lengths

Makes

Everything we eat these days, we question whether we can turn it into a cheesecake. Sometimes it works, sometimes it doesn't!

There is never a dull day in Pleesecake world.

Experimenting with different flavours – ones that you might not think would work – is something we love to do in the Pleesecake kitchen.

Don't be scared by the idea of a savoury cheesecake

– these are our favourite combos and they really work!

RUBY MURRAY MINIS

This is not a joke, repeat, this is not a joke! Some may say this is crazy, some may say it shouldn't work, but they would all be very wrong! We are both very partial to a Ruby Murray (curry) and a few beers on a Friday, who isn't?! So we set ourselves a challenge to turn our Friday night curry into one of our cheesecake recipes. It's a powerful statement and memorable, to say the least. But it really does work, so give it a go!

Preheat the oven to 200°C (400°F/gas mark 6). Line a baking sheet with baking (parchment) paper and set two 10cm (4 inch) ring cutters on it.

For the base, mix the onion with the curry powder, cumin seeds and ground coriander. Divide this mixture into two.

Crack the egg into a bowl and whisk slightly. Pour the flour into another bowl. Drop the first portion of onion into the egg, from there into the flour and finally into a ring cutter, pressing down firmly to form the bhaji base (you don't want any gaps). Repeat for the other portion of onions. Place in the oven for 12–15 minutes.

For the filling, put the olive oil in a frying pan, followed by the paneer and chickpeas (garbanzo beans). Add the curry powder, chilli flakes (crushed chili pepper), allspice, cumin seeds and a pinch of salt and pepper, and fry off for 5–6 minutes. Once golden brown, add the cream cheese and spinach, and cook for a further 4–5 minutes.

Remove the bhajis from the oven and spoon the paneer mixture equally on top of each base. Pat down and leave to cool. Cover with cling film (plastic wrap) until ready to serve.

When you're ready to serve, whack them back in the oven for 3–4 minutes to warm through. Once warmed, remove from the oven and place on a plate. Remove the ring carefully (don't mess it up now). Finish off with a scoop of yogurt, a dollop of mango chutney, a few mini poppadums and a sprinkle of fresh mint.

You'll need: 2 x 10cm (4 inch) ring cutters

Base
1 red onion, sliced
1 tbsp curry powder
1 tbsp cumin seeds
1 tbsp ground coriander
1 egg
100g (¾ cup) plain (all-purpose) flour

Filling
10ml (2 tsp) olive oil
110g (3¾oz) paneer cheese, sliced
120g (scant 1 cup) canned chickpeas (garbanzo beans), drained and rinsed
1 tbsp curry powder
1 tbsp chilli flakes (crushed chili pepper)
1 tsp ground allspice
1 tsp cumin seeds
140g (⅔ cup) cream cheese
50g (1¾oz) spinach
salt and pepper

Topping
2 tbsp Greek yogurt
2 tbsp mango chutney
mini poppadums
small handful of fresh mint leaves

Serves

WINGIN' IT

From day one we have had to 'wing' a lot of situations. We both love a good chicken wing and you can't beat a good blue cheese dip. So, cometh the hour, cometh the man, we thought, why not stick a blue cheese-inspired Pleesecake on the plate, with beautiful, succulent, juicy chicken wings on the side? You have to try this one, it's a life changer!

Preheat your oven to 200°C (400°F/gas mark 6). Start by marinating your wings with a good-quality buffalo hot sauce, or BBQ sauce if you don't like it on the spicy side. Massage the wings in a bowl to get the flavours penetrating. Cover the bowl and stick it in the fridge while you crack on.

While your wings are marinating, let's get on with the blue cheese Pleesecake. Put your beaten egg in one bowl, your flour in another and get a roasting tin (pan) oiled and ready to stick the onions in. Get dipping, onions into egg, then flour, shake off the excess flour and then straight into the tin. Once done, put them in the oven for 10–15 minutes – you want them nice and crispy – sogginess just won't do!

While your onions are crisping up nicely, get on with the filling. Chop your blue cheese up into nice little chunks, stick that in your bowl with the cream cheese, give it a sprinkle of chives, season with salt and pepper, and mix it all together.

Get your onions out of the oven and let them cool down fully. Divide the onions equally between the moulds, pressing down firmly to make your base. Spoon in the blue cheese filling, again pressing down firmly to make sure there are no air bubbles. Stick it in the fridge to chill for 30 minutes.

Right, wing time – stick the wings in a baking tray and get 'em in that oven for 25–30 minutes (we like them in there a bit longer so they crisp up). You've got a bit of free time now, so have a couple of swifties while you're waiting.

After 30 minutes, your wings are starting to look like the things dreams are made of! Pop your blue cheese Pleesecakes out of the mould, and place effortlessly on a plate or large serving board. Get your wings around the Pleesecake beauty. Drizzle your wings with a bit more buffalo sauce and scatter over the spring onions (scallions), chillies and coriander (cilantro). Stick some celery in a cup.

Bosh, there you have it – WINGIN' IT.

You'll need: 4 mini cheesecake moulds or a mini cheesecake tray (12 compartments)

Base
1 egg, beaten
150g (scant 1¼ cups) plain (all-purpose) flour
2 onions, very thinly sliced

Filling
200g (7oz) blue cheese
280g (10oz) cream cheese
2 tbsp chopped chives
salt and pepper

Toppings
1kg (2lb 4oz) chicken wings
buffalo sauce or barbecue sauce
2 spring onions (scallions), thinly sliced
2 red chillies, deseeded and thinly sliced
handful of coriander (cilantro) leaves
2 or 3 celery sticks, to serve (optional)

Serves 👤👤👤👤

SWEET DREAMS ARE MADE OF BRIE & CRANBERRY

We've doubled up on the cheese on this little beaut, because you can never have too much cheese, ay! It's a classic flavour combo and we nicked it from our first Christmas range, which we released in December 2017. It's not everyone's cup of tea, but the gooey salty Brie and the juicy cranberries are sooo decent!

Whizz the crackers to a fine crumb in a food processor (stick 'em in a sandwich bag and bash with a rolling pin if you haven't got a processor). Add the melted butter and give it a good stir to make sure that all the biscuit is nicely coated, then mix in the seeds. Divide evenly between the moulds, press down gently to make your base and place in the fridge for 30 minutes to firm up.

In a bowl, mix together the cream cheese, Brie, cranberry sauce and thyme, with a pinch of salt and pepper. Once you've given it a good mix, spoon it into the moulds and level off with a palette knife. Stick 'em back in the fridge for at least 2 hours to set.

Once set, remove from the fridge and take them out of the moulds. To decorate, simply scoop on a dollop of cranberry sauce, a healthy chunk of Brie, some fresh cranberries, a few walnuts, a few redcurrants, if using, and a sprig of fresh thyme. Enjoy! This is great to serve over indulgent festive periods!

You'll need: 4 mini cheesecake moulds or a mini cheesecake tray (12 compartments)

Base
120g (4¼oz) cream (savoury) crackers
40g (3 tbsp) unsalted butter, melted
40g (scant ⅓ cup) mixed seeds

Filling
400g (14oz) cream cheese
180g (6¼oz) Brie, chopped into small chunks
120g (¾ cup) cranberry sauce
leaves picked from 3 fresh thyme sprigs, plus extra for topping
salt and pepper

Topping
80g (¼ cup) cranberry sauce
160g (5½oz) Brie
20g (3 tbsp) fresh cranberries
a small sprig of redcurrants (optional)
20g (3 tbsp) walnuts

Serves 👤👤👤👤

MELON & PARMA HAM CUPS

These little cups of joy pack a right old punch. With just five ingredients it's such a simple recipe – quick and easy to make. You can have these as canapés, as a starter or even a mid-week light dinner with a side salad. It's definitely one of our favourites with the creamy cheese and salty Parma ham. It's a classic match made in heaven. We guarantee you're going to love these!

Preheat the oven to 180°C (350°F/gas mark 4). Line six moulds with layers of the Parma ham and sage leaves to create a small basket. Place in the oven for 5 minutes, then set aside to cool.

In a bowl, mix together the cream cheese and finely chopped thyme and sage, along with a pinch of salt and pepper.

Once the Parma ham baskets have cooled, remove from the moulds and spoon in the cheese mix, compressing it down with the back of a spoon. Using a tablespoon, scoop out chunks of melon and place on top of each basket. Finish off with a few sprigs of thyme and a few sage leaves before serving.

You'll need: bitesize mini cheesecake tray (20 compartments)

Base
200g (7oz) Parma ham
18 fresh sage leaves

Filling
70g (1/3 cup) cream cheese
leaves from a few sprigs fresh thyme, finely chopped
small bunch of fresh sage, leaves finely chopped
salt and pepper

Topping
200g (7oz) melon
fresh thyme sprigs
sage leaves

Makes 🧍🧍🧍🧍🧍

BEETROOT & FETA MINIS

If you're looking for a completely original idea for a starter, these beetroot and feta mini Pleesecakes might just be the answer! You've got to like feta and you've got to like beetroot (although sweet potato or butternut squash would work instead). Either way we've stepped outside the box to bring you a dish that's fun, looks great and tastes amazing!

Blitz the crackers to a coarse crumb in a food processor (stick 'em in a sandwich bag and bash with a rolling pin if you haven't got a processor). Add the melted butter, and give it a good stir to make sure that all the crackers are nicely coated, then mix in the seeds. Divide evenly between the moulds, press down gently to make your base and place in the fridge for 30 minutes to firm up.

Beat the cream cheese and feta cheese together. Whizz the beetroot into a fine paste in a food processor. Add the beetroot to the cheese mixture along with a healthy pinch of salt and pepper, and mix together thoroughly. Spoon into the moulds and level off with a palette knife. Whack 'em in the fridge for at least 2 hours to set.

Once firm, remove from the fridge and take them out of the moulds. To top these beauts, mix the rocket (arugula) with the balsamic vinegar and olive oil. Put the feta onto each cheesecake. Scrunch the salad into three equal balls and place on top of each cheesecake. Add a sprinkle of seeds and you're ready to serve and WOW your guests!

You'll need: 3 mini cheesecake moulds or a mini cheesecake tray (12 compartments)

Base
95g (3¼oz) cream (savoury) crackers
30g (2 tbsp) unsalted butter, melted
30g (4 tbsp) mixed seeds

Filling
160g (¾ cup) cream cheese
40g (1½oz) feta cheese
100g (3½oz) cooked beetroot
salt and pepper

Topping
45g (1½oz) rocket (arugula)
20g (2½ tbsp) mixed seeds
30g (1oz) feta cheese, finely chopped
10ml (2 tsp) balsamic vinegar
4ml (scant 1 tsp) olive oil

Serves

black forest gateau

ETON
MESS

**CHEESECAKE
& APPLE PIE
LOVE CHILD**

LEMON MERINGUE

MORE S'MORES PLEASE CAKE

HOT-CRO
BUNS

**THE CHOC
ORANGE
PLEESECAKE**

honey, i'

EASTER
EGGS

CHILLI-
WILLY
CHOCOLATE

PIE
SS

comb!
MINCE PIES

MIXED BERRY
PLEESECAKE

summer fruits fun

HOT-CROSS BUNS

At Easter time, the chocolate egg is the go-to dessert for both young and old – we all know that parents are nicking the kids' Easter eggs when they're not looking. But the hot cross bun is also around at this time of the year so we've created this dessert. It has all the flavours of a spicy fruity bun and the richness and indulgence of a cheesecake – perfect to avoid fights. Plus, you can make it all year round!

Whizz the ginger biscuits to a fine crumb in a food processor (stick 'em in a sandwich bag and bash with a rolling pin if you haven't got a processor). Add the melted butter, and give it a good stir to make sure that all the biscuit is nicely coated, then mix in the orange zest, cinnamon and raisins. Divide evenly between the moulds, press down gently to make your base and place in the fridge for 30 minutes to firm up.

Beat the cream cheese and sugar together. Add the raisins, cinnamon and orange zest, and mix together thoroughly. Whip the cream until you have stiff peaks and fold it gently into the mix. Spoon into the moulds and level off with a palette knife. Stick it in the freezer for at least 1 hour to set.

Once set, remove from the freezer and take out of the moulds. Dust the tops with cocoa powder in the shape of a cross (a piece of baking/parchment paper is ideal to create nice straight edges). Voila – a banging, indulgent little dessert!

Allow to defrost in the fridge for 1–2 hours before serving.

You'll need: 2 mini cheesecake moulds or a mini cheesecake tray (12 compartments)

Base
75g (2½oz) ginger nut biscuits
15g (1 tbsp) unsalted butter, melted
zest of ½ orange
½ tsp ground cinnamon
20g (2 tbsp) raisins

Filling
200g (scant 1 cup) cream cheese
40g (scant ¼ cup) caster (superfine) sugar
30g (3 tbsp) raisins
1 tsp ground cinnamon
zest of ½ orange
80ml (⅓ cup) double (heavy) cream

Topping
cocoa powder, for dusting

Serves 👤👤

EASTER EGGS

Now we all know that, more often than not, there's always a few Easter eggs floating about three weeks after Easter. Don't let them go to waste – instead, fill them with cheesecake! Yep, that's right, we've discovered that Easter eggs are a banging alternative to a bowl or cup as a base for a Pleesecake! Genius, we know! It's double simple and a great one for everyone to get involved with! We made this up on our first Easter and people went mad for it. We called it the 'Easter egg board'.

Carefully break the Easter egg into two halves – one for each person – and place on a tray. Whizz the biscuits to a fine crumb in a food processor (stick 'em in a sandwich bag and bash with a rolling pin if you haven't got a processor). Divide evenly between the two egg halves. Press down very gently – be careful you don't want to crack that egg! Place in the fridge while you crack on with the filling.

Beat the cream cheese and sugar together. Add the hazelnut chocolate spread (feel free to use an alternative flavour, but we think this works well!) and mix together thoroughly. Whip the cream until you have stiff peaks, and fold it gently into the mix with the vanilla bean paste to give a marbled effect. You're looking for a silky sexy mixture.

Remove the egg halves from the fridge and scoop in the mixture evenly. Smooth off with the back of a spoon and whack them back in the fridge for 1–2 hours to set.

Once set, get the egg halves out of the fridge. It's now time to get creative. We've suggested a few toppings, but if there's something that works for you, we fully endorse smashing it on there! There's no right or wrong, so get the whole team involved and make something delicious and incredible looking!

Base
1 hollow milk or dark chocolate Easter egg of your choice, about 100g (3¹/₂oz)
100g (3¹/₂oz) plain digestive biscuits

Filling
200g (scant 1 cup) cream cheese
20g (³/₄oz) caster (superfine) sugar
40g (1¹/₂oz) hazelnut chocolate spread
50ml (scant ¹/₄ cup) double (heavy) cream
5g (1 tsp) vanilla bean paste

Toppings
mini chocolate eggs, chocolate bunnies, chocolate buttons, about 400g (14oz) in total

Serves 👨👨

BLACK FOREST GATEAU

A classic cake idea – so we nicked it and turned it into a Pleesecake. It uses simple ingredients and is even simpler to make. It's great during the colder months with a glass of mulled wine! This one speaks for itself and looks so good, you're bound to impress!

Whizz the biscuits to a fine crumb in a food processor (stick 'em in a sandwich bag and bash with a rolling pin if you haven't got a processor). Add the melted butter and give it a good stir to make sure that all the biscuit is nicely coated, then mix in the milk and dark choc drops. Pour into the cake tin (pan) and press down gently and evenly to make your base. Level off around the edge with the back of a spoon and place in the freezer for 15 minutes to firm up.

Beat the cream cheese and sugar together. Add the cherry compote and cherry liqueur, and mix together thoroughly. Whip the cream until you have stiff peaks, and fold it gently into the mix. Spoon into the cake tin and level off with a palette knife. Run your forefinger and thumb around the rim of the tin to create a professional finish and tap the tin gently on a hard surface to remove any air bubbles. Stick it in the freezer for at least 2 hours to set.

Once set, remove from the freezer, take it out of the tin and we're ready to decorate.

To make the chocolate drizzle, blitz the dark and milk chocolate in the food processor into a coarse crumb and whack it in a heatproof bowl. Heat the cream until piping hot (but not bubbling). Pour 75ml (scant ⅓ cup) of the cream onto the chocolate gradually, stirring as you go, making sure the consistency is smooth and lump-free. Then drizzle it onto the cake, starting in the middle and using the back of a spoon to gently encourage the chocolate over the edge.

Working fast so that you can finish the toppings while the chocolate is still wet, first mix together the compote and liqueur in a bowl. Next, whip the remaining cream to soft peaks. Pipe some cream all over the cake, followed by a sprinkling of fresh cherries, spoonfuls of compote/liqueur mix, and finally some glacé (candied) cherries and dark choc drops. Another banger!

Allow to defrost in the fridge for 3–5 hours before serving.

You'll need: 18cm/7 inch deep springform cake tin (pan)

Base
320g (11¼oz) double chocolate digestive biscuits
30g (2 tbsp) unsalted butter, melted
15g (¼oz) milk chocolate drops
15g (¼oz) dark chocolate drops

Filling
720g (1lb 9oz) cream cheese
80g (generous ⅓ cup) caster (superfine) sugar
350g (12¼oz) cherry compote
50ml (scant ¼ cup) cherry liqueur
250ml (1 cup) double (heavy) cream

Topping
50g (1¾oz) dark chocolate
50g (1¾oz) milk chocolate
175ml (¾ cup) double (heavy) cream
125g (4½oz) cherry compote
15ml (1 tbsp) cherry liqueur
100g (3½oz) cherries
100g (3½oz) Italian glacé (candied) Morello cherries
15g (½oz) dark chocolate drops

Serves

THE CHOC ORANGE PLEESECAKE

What can be better than the combination of chocolate and orange? It's such a banging fusion of flavours! Putting these flavours into a Pleesecake was inevitable. It's simple, double double easy to make and tastes real sexy!

Whizz the double chocolate digestive biscuits to a fine crumb in a food processor (or stick 'em in a sandwich bag and bash with a rolling pin if you haven't got a processor). Add the melted butter, and give it a good stir to make sure that all the ingredients are coated nicely, then mix in the orange zest and dark choc drops. Divide evenly between the moulds, press down gently to make your bases and place in the freezer for 15 minutes.

Beat the cream cheese and sugar together. Add the chocolate spread, orange zest and orange essence, and mix together thoroughly.

Whip the cream until you have stiff peaks and fold it gently into the mix, along with the dark choc drops. Spoon into the moulds and level off with a palette knife. Place in the freezer for at least 3 hours to firm up.

Make the chocolate shards. Line a baking sheet with baking (parchment) paper. Melt the dark chocolate in the microwave or a heatproof bowl set over a pan of simmering water, then spread it out all over the baking sheet (roughly 2mm/⅛ inch thick). Grate the orange zest over the wet chocolate and sprinkle with a few drops of orange essence, then place in the freezer for 30 minutes to set.

Once the cakes are set, remove from the freezer and take them out of the moulds. To make the chocolate drizzle, blitz the dark chocolate (not drops) into a coarse crumb and put it in a heatproof bowl. Heat the cream until piping hot (not bubbling) and pour onto the chocolate gradually, stirring, making sure the consistency is smooth and lump-free. Drizzle it onto the cake, starting in the middle and using the back of a spoon to encourage the chocolate over the edge.

Working fast while the chocolate drizzle is still wet, remove the chocolate from the freezer and break into shards. Jab the shards randomly into the cake. A final zesting of orange and a sprinkle of dark choc drops, then stick it back in the freezer to set.

Allow to defrost in the fridge for 1–2 hours before serving.

You'll need: 4 mini cheesecake moulds or a mini cheesecake tray (12 compartments)

Base
160g (5½oz) double chocolate digestive biscuits
25g (1¾ tbsp) unsalted butter, melted
zest of 1 orange
40g (1½oz) dark chocolate drops

Filling
320g (11¼oz) cream cheese
80g (generous ⅓ cup) caster (superfine) sugar
180g (generous ½ cup) chocolate spread
zest of 2 oranges
4 tsp orange essence
160ml (scant ⅔ cup) double (heavy) cream
40g (1½oz) dark chocolate drops

Chocolate shards
100g (3½oz) dark chocolate
zest of ½ orange
5ml (1 tsp) orange essence

Toppings
100g (3½oz) dark chocolate
75ml (⅓ cup) double (heavy) cream
zest of ½ orange
20g (½oz) dark chocolate drops

Serves

MINCE PIES

There are so many lovely seasonal flavours when it comes to Christmas time. It was hard to choose our favourites to put in this book. This one made the cut without a shadow of a doubt. I mean, have you ever had a mince pie cheesecake, with a mince pie base? Maybe this Christmas, instead of making mince pies, you could make these banging mince pie cheesecakes for everyone! A nice little gift idea for friends and family too!

For the base, simply whizz up the mince pies and digestive biscuits in a food processor until you have a fine crumb. Add the melted butter and give it a good stir to make sure that everything is nicely coated. Divide evenly between the moulds, press down gently to make your base and place in the fridge for 30 minutes to firm up.

Beat the cream cheese and sugar together. Add the mincemeat, cinnamon, nutmeg and mixed spice, and mix together thoroughly. Whip the cream until you have stiff peaks and fold it gently into the mix. Spoon into the moulds and level off with a palette knife. Stick 'em back in the fridge for at least 2 hours to set.

Once set, remove from the fridge and take them out of the moulds. Top with a spoonful of mincemeat, a dollop of brandy cream, if you like, a mini mince pie or some Christmassy chocolates and a candy cane, and you can also add a sprinkle of crushed meringue for that authentic snow effect! Get stuck in, this one's double deece!

You'll need: 6 mini cheesecake
moulds or a mini cheesecake tray
(12 compartments)

Base
180g (6¼oz) mince pies
90g (3¼oz) plain digestive biscuits
30g (2 tbsp) unsalted butter, melted

Filling
600g (1lb 5oz) cream cheese
120g (⅔ cup) caster (superfine)
sugar
240g (8½oz) mincemeat
3 tsp ground cinnamon
1 tsp freshly grated nutmeg
3 tsp mixed (apple pie) spice
240ml (1 cup) double (heavy) cream

Topping
180g (6¼oz) mincemeat
40g (1½oz) brandy cream, optional
6 x mini mince pies (30g/1oz each)
or Christmassy chocolates
6 x candy canes
10g (¼oz) meringue, crushed
(optional)

Serves

ETON MESS

Here's another classic dessert that we've adapted. This one's a real looker and it was one of our first creations back when we started. It was during an experimental stage – we were trying to create amazing-looking cakes, but keeping it simple at the same time. It's such a pretty dessert and so fun and easy to make.

Whizz the biscuits to a fine crumb in a food processor (stick 'em in a sandwich bag and bash with a rolling pin if you haven't got a processor). Add the melted butter and give it a good stir to make sure that all the biscuit is nicely coated, then mix in the freeze-dried strawberries and crushed meringue. Pour into the cake tin (pan) and press down gently and evenly to make your base. Level off around the edge with the back of a spoon and place in the freezer for 15 minutes to firm up.

Beat the cream cheese and 75g (6 tbsp) sugar together. Blitz 100g (½ cup) of the strawberries with the remaining sugar into a purée and add to the mix. Finely chop the remaining strawberries and add them as well, and mix together thoroughly. Whip the cream until you have soft peaks and fold it gently into the mix. Spoon into the cake tin, level off with a palette knife and run your forefinger and thumb around the rim of the tin to create a professional finish. Then poke in the chunks of meringue and flakes so that some are completely submerged and some stick out the top. Tap the tin gently on a hard surface to remove any air bubbles and stick it back in the freezer for at least 3 hours to set.

When you are ready to decorate, remove the cake from the freezer and take it out of the tin. For the white chocolate drizzle, blitz the white chocolate into a coarse crumb and whack it in a heatproof bowl. Heat the cream until piping hot (but not bubbling). Pour the cream onto the chocolate gradually, stirring as you go, until completely melted, smooth and lump-free. Then drizzle it onto the cake, starting in the middle and using the back of a spoon to gently encourage the chocolate over the edge.

While the chocolate is still wet, add the remaining toppings. First, the fresh strawberries, then the flakey chocolate, followed by the meringues, buttons and freeze-dried strawberries. Some flowers or mint add colour.

Allow to defrost in the fridge for 3–4 hours before serving.

You'll need: 20cm (8 inch) deep springform cake tin (pan)

Base
360g (12³/₄oz) plain digestive biscuits
80g (⅓ cup) unsalted butter
3 tbsp freeze-dried strawberries
20g (³/₄oz) meringue, crushed

Filling
750g (11lb 10oz) cream cheese
100g (½ cup) caster (superfine) sugar
240g (1²/₃ cup) strawberries, hulled
250ml (1 cup) double (heavy) cream
30g (1oz) meringues, broken into large chunks
80g (2³/₄oz) milk chocolate flakes, halved widthways

Topping
90g (3¹/₄oz) white chocolate
90ml (generous ⅓ cup) double (heavy) cream
230g (2¹/₃ cups) fresh strawberries, halved lengthways
80g (2³/₄oz) flakey milk chocolate bars, halved widthways
25g (1oz) meringues, crushed
1 tbsp white chocolate buttons
2 tbsp freeze-dried strawberries
edible flowers or fresh mint sprigs

Serves

For us the perfect Pleesecake has got to start with a

DCB (double-choc base),

a banoffee filling
with fudge pieces,

choc drizzle,

then loaded with all our fave chocolate. Might as well chuck some sweets on there as well.

Fresh and dried fruits also make good toppings, as well as good old chocolate sauce. We like to go for a 10-second no-break drizzle!

The best tip we can possibly give you on decorating your own Pleesecakes is to have fun and get as much on there as you can. If you can see a gap, you ain't got enough on there –

so whack a Choccy B in there!

If you're really struggling for inspo then get on the Instagram and get Pleesecake inspired!!!

HONEY, I'M COMB!

This takes about 10 minutes to make. A very worthwhile 10 minutes in our eyes, given the results and the deliciousness you're going to get from this absolute banger of a dessert! Double quick, double tasty, double win! A lovely little celebratory midweeker!!!

Smash up the biscuits and honeycomb, leaving it fairly chunky. Spoon into the glasses and set aside.

Beat the cream cheese and sugar together. Stir in the honey and honeycomb. Whip the cream until you have stiff peaks and fold it gently into the mix. Melt the milk chocolate in the microwave or a heatproof bowl set over a pan of simmering water. Let it cool a bit, then pour it into the mix and stir lightly to create a swirled effect.

Spoon into the glasses and add the topping honeycomb. Melt the topping chocolate as above and finish off with an indulgent drizzle of melted chocolate. You're ready to tuck into heaven!

You'll need: 2 glass tumblers

Base
80g (2³/₄oz) plain digestive biscuit
20g (³/₄oz) honeycomb

Filling
160g (³/₄ cup) cream cheese
20g (1 tbsp) caster (superfine) sugar
2 tbsp honey
60g (2¹/₄oz) honeycomb, crushed
70ml (generous ¹/₄ cup) double (heavy) cream
50g (1³/₄oz) milk chocolate

Topping
40g (1¹/₂oz) honeycomb, broken into pieces
60g (2¹/₄oz) milk chocolate

Serves 👤👤

SUMMER FRUITS FUN

This is by far one of the more traditional cheesecakes in the book. It's a summer belter – when you've stuffed your face with loads of heavy BBQ food, all you want is a nice refreshing, fruity cap-off to send you into a food coma! It looks great and livens the palate up on a hot sweltering day (it's likely to be relevant to our international readers located in hot destinations, because Britain rarely has sweltering days!).

Whizz the biscuits to a fine crumb in a food processor (stick 'em in a sandwich bag and bash with a rolling pin if you haven't got a processor). Add the melted butter and give it a good stir to make sure that all the biscuit is nicely coated, then mix in the fresh raspberries and lemon zest. Pour into the cake tin (pan) and press down gently and evenly to make your base. Level off around the edge with the back of a spoon and place in the freezer for 15 minutes to firm up.

Beat the cream cheese and 90g (7 tbsp) of the sugar together. Blitz 100g ($^2/_3$ cup) of the raspberries with 2$^1/_2$ tbsp of the sugar to make a purée. Blitz the passion fruit with 1 tbsp of the sugar and then the mango with the remaining sugar. Add the purées, remaining whole raspberries, lemon zest and juice to the cream cheese, and mix together thoroughly. Whip the cream until you have stiff peaks and fold it gently into the mix. Spoon into the cake tin and level off with a palette knife. Stick it back in the freezer for at least 3 hours to set.

For the coulis, simply whizz up the mixed berries and sugar.

Once the cake is set, remove from the freezer and take it out of the cake tin and we're ready to decorate. For the topping, spoon on the coulis, then pile on the mixed fruit. A few sprigs of fresh mint and a final zesting of lemon, and that's a winner right there!

Allow to defrost in the fridge for 3–4 hours before serving.

Serves 👤👤👤👤👤👤👤👤 – 👤👤

You'll need: 20cm (8 inch) deep springform cake tin (pan)

Base
225g (8oz) shortbread biscuits
135g (4$^3/_4$oz) plain digestive biscuits
40g (3 tbsp) unsalted butter, melted
45g ($^1/_3$ cup) fresh raspberries
zest of 1 lemon

Filling
900g (2lb) cream cheese
175g (generous $^3/_4$ cup) caster (superfine) sugar
150g (1 cup) raspberries
100g (3$^1/_2$oz) passion fruit
100g (3$^1/_2$oz) mango
zest of 1 lemon
50ml (scant $^1/_4$ cup) lemon juice
180ml ($^3/_4$ cup) double (heavy) cream

Mixed berry coulis
200g (1$^1/_2$ cups) mixed berries
30g (2$^1/_2$ tbsp) caster (superfine) sugar

Topping
500–600g (1lb 2oz–1lb 5oz) fresh mixed fruit
fresh mint sprigs
zest of $^1/_2$ lemon

MIXED BERRY PLEESECAKE

Sometimes, keeping things simple is essential. We know most people have mad busy lives and scheduling in time to make dessert just doesn't happen. This berry wonder is simple but packs a punch with your favourite fruity flavours! From base to topping, you'll be well pleased you chose this one for simplicity alone!

Whizz the biscuits to a fine crumb in a food processor (stick 'em in a sandwich bag and bash with a rolling pin if you haven't got a processor). Add the melted butter and give it a good stir to make sure that the biscuit is nicely coated, then mix in the choc chips. Pour into the cake tin (pan) and press down gently and evenly to make your base. Level off around the edge with the back of a spoon and place in the freezer for 15 minutes to firm up.

Beat the cream cheese and sugar together. Add the compote and the blueberries and mix together thoroughly. Whip the cream until you have stiff peaks and fold it gently into the mix. You should have a nice silky appearance. Spoon into the cake tin, level off with a palette knife and then run your forefinger and thumb around the rim of the tin to create a professional finish. Tap the tin gently on a hard surface to remove any air bubbles and stick it in the freezer for at least 3 hours to set.

Once set, remove from the freezer and take it out of the tin. Spoon on the compote as a sticky base for all the fruit. With no right or wrong way, use your creativity to randomly place the fruit on top. A few dark choc drops and you're ready to go.

Allow to defrost in the fridge for 3-4 hours before serving.

You'll need: 18cm/7 inch deep springform cake tin (pan)

Base
320g (11¼oz) double chocolate digestive biscuits
30g (2 tbsp) unsalted butter, melted
15g (4 tsp) dark chocolate chips
15g (4 tsp) milk chocolate chips

Filling
720g (1lb 9oz) cream cheese
80g (generous ⅓ cup) caster (superfine) sugar
200g (7oz) blueberry compote
100g (¾ cup) blueberries
200ml (generous ¾ cup) double (heavy) cream

Toppings
400g (14oz) mixed berry compote
400–600g (14oz–1lb 5oz) mixed berries (cherries, blackberries, blueberries)
20g (¾oz) dark chocolate drops

Serves

CHILLI-WILLY CHOCOLATE

We're here to spice up the cheesecake world and bring you something that's going to heat up that dinner party or family BBQ! We both love a bit of spice, and we both love a dessert – why not combine the two and have the best of both worlds in one dish?! This may not be for everyone, but if you like chilli, give it a go, it really does work. It's definitely the answer to spicing up your dessert life! HOT HOT HOT!!!

Let's kick things off by whizzing up the biscuits to a fine crumb in a food processor (stick 'em in a sandwich bag and bash with a rolling pin if you haven't got a processor). Add the melted butter and give it a good stir, making sure that all the biscuit is nicely coated, then mix in the choc chips. Pour into the cake tin (pan) and press down gently and evenly to make your base. Level off around the edge with the back of a spoon and place in the freezer for 15 minutes to firm up.

Next, make the chilli chocolate shards. Line a baking sheet with baking (parchment) paper. Melt the dark chocolate in the microwave or a heatproof bowl set over a pan of simmering water, then spread it out all over the baking sheet (roughly 2mm/$\frac{1}{8}$ inch thick). While the chocolate is still wet, sprinkle the chilli flakes and sea salt over the top. Place in the freezer for 30 minutes to set.

Beat the cream cheese and sugar together. Melt the dark and milk chocolate in the microwave or a heatproof bowl set over a pan of simmering water. Let it cool a bit, then add to the cheese, along with the chocolate spread, chilli flakes and fresh chilli, and mix together thoroughly. Whip the cream until you have stiff peaks and fold it gently into the mix. Spoon into the cake tin and level off with a palette knife. Run your forefinger and thumb around the rim of the tin to create a professional finish. While the cake is still soft, remove the chilli chocolate from the freezer and break up into shards. Stick them in randomly all over the surface of the cake. Tap the tin gently on a hard surface to remove any air bubbles and place back in the freezer for at least 3 hours to set.

Once set, remove from the freezer and take it out of the tin. Spread with the compote and cover with the raspberries. Allow to defrost in the fridge for 3–4 hours before serving.

You'll need: 18cm/7 inch deep springform cake tin (pan)

Base
275g (9$\frac{3}{4}$oz) double chocolate digestive biscuits
45g (3 tbsp) butter, melted
10g (1 tbsp) dark chocolate chips
10g (1 tbsp) milk chocolate chips

Chilli chocolate shards
200g (7oz) dark chocolate
1 tbsp chilli flakes (crushed chili pepper)
pinch of sea salt

Filling
775g (1lb 11oz) cream cheese
80g (generous $\frac{1}{3}$ cup) caster sugar
55g (2oz) dark chocolate
55g (2oz) milk chocolate
200g ($\frac{2}{3}$ cup) chocolate spread
1$\frac{1}{2}$ tbsp chilli flakes (crushed chili pepper)
$\frac{1}{2}$ red chilli, deseeded and sliced
75ml (scant $\frac{1}{3}$ cup) double (heavy) cream

Topping
50g (1$\frac{3}{4}$oz) raspberry compote
50g (generous $\frac{1}{2}$ cup) fresh raspberries

Serves 👤👤👤👤👤👤 - 👤👤

LEMON MERINGUE PIE

This lemon meringue pie cheesecake is really simple, tastes amazing and looks the nuts. We challenge you to have a go at this one. We'd love to see some of your creations – #lemonmeringuepleesecake. Get posting and tagging us on Insta!

Whizz the digestive biscuits to a fine crumb in a food processor (stick 'em in a sandwich bag and bash with a rolling pin if you haven't got a processor). Add the melted butter and give it a good stir to make sure that all the biscuit is nicely coated, then mix in the lemon zest. Pour into the cake tin (pan), press down gently in the middle to make your base, and push the biscuit up the sides to make a wall around the edge of the tin. Level off around the edge with the back of a spoon and place in the fridge for 15 minutes to firm up.

Beat the cream cheese and sugar together. Add the lemon zest and juice, and lemon essence, and mix together thoroughly. Whip the cream until you have stiff peaks and fold it gently into the mix. Set aside while you make the meringue.

To make the Italian meringue, whisk the egg whites and cream of tartar in a mixer until you are nearly at the stiff peak stage, then switch off the mixer. In a saucepan, heat the sugar and water over a low heat until the sugar has dissolved. Once dissolved, turn up the heat slightly and simmer until the syrup reaches 118°C (245°F). Remove from heat and turn the mixer back on to full power, slowly adding the syrup. Whisk until the eggs are firm, silky and shiny in appearance. Set aside while you assemble the cake.

Remove the base from the freezer and spoon in the lemon curd, spreading it out evenly. Next, spoon on the cheese mixture and level off with a palette knife. For the topping, spoon the meringue all over the cake, then use a spoon to swirl it. Using a domestic blow torch, torch the meringue peaks until golden brown. A final zesting of lemon and the cake is ready to be devoured.

You'll need: 20cm (8 inch) deep springform cake tin (pan)

Base
380g (13½oz) plain digestive biscuits
110g (½ cup) unsalted butter, melted
zest of 2 lemons

Filling
420g (15oz) cream cheese
90g (½ cup) caster (superfine) sugar
zest and juice of 2 lemons
5ml (1 tsp) lemon essence
90ml (generous ⅓ cup) double (heavy) cream
280g (10oz) lemon curd

Italian meringue topping
3 egg whites
5g (1½ tsp) cream of tartar
150g (¾ cup) caster sugar
75ml (⅓ cup) water
zest of 1 lemon

Serves 👤👤👤👤👤👤👤 – 👤👤

MORE S'MORES PLEASE CAKE

We're not going to lie to you, but we've gone double indulgent on this one! It's highly recommended that you don't consume this on a daily basis, or even a weekly or monthly basis – but it's so much fun to assemble and there's no skill involved whatsoever, so everyone can have a go! Also, if you can't be bothered to make your son or daughter's birthday cake – get them to make it themselves!

Preheat the oven to 160°C (320°F/gas mark 3). First make the base cookie. Add the water to the cookie mix and bring together to form a dough. Spread over the entire base of one of the cake tins (pans), making sure it's level for an even bake. Repeat with the cookie mix and water for the topping, spreading it over the base of the other cake tin (it should be half as thick). Whack them both in the oven for 10–12 minutes. Once golden brown, remove from the oven and release the springform tin sides (keeping the base on) and place the cookies on a rack. The thinner topping cookie should be nice and crispy, and the thicker base cookie should still be a bit gooey. While still hot and soft, stuff the large marshmallows randomly across the surface of the thicker base cookie.

For the filling, beat the cream cheese and sugar together. Add the vanilla paste and mix thoroughly. Whip the cream until you have stiff peaks and fold it gently into the mix.

When the cookies are completely cool, you can remove the bases. You should be left with two 20cm (8 inch) cookies – one deep and marshmallow-encrusted (the base) and the other shallower. Spoon the cheese mixture randomly onto the base cookie and sprinkle with the mini marshmallows and choc chips. Melt the milk and dark chocolate in the microwave or a heatproof bowl set over a pan of simmering water. Drizzle it all over the base cookie and filling.

Top with the second cookie, aking it up into large chunks as you stick it on top of the filling. Decorate with small marshmallows and thin shavings of the milk chocolate. Melt a few of the marshmallows and drizzle over the top, if you like. Blitz the Oreo to a fine crumb in a food processor and give the cake a final sprinkle, and it's ready to be plonked in the middle of the table to be annihilated.

You'll need: 2 x 20cm (8 inch) deep springform cake tins (pans)

Base
60ml (¼ cup) water
400g (14oz) cookie mix
130g (4½oz) large marshmallows

Filling
300g (1⅓ cup) cream cheese
30g (2½ tbsp) caster (superfine) sugar
15g (1 tbsp) vanilla bean paste
50ml (scant ¼ cup) double (heavy) cream
30g (¾ cup) mini marshmallows
30g (2¾ tbsp) dark chocolate chips
100g (3½oz) milk chocolate
100g (3½oz) dark chocolate

Topping
200g (7oz) cookie mix
30ml (2 tbsp) water
20g (½ cup) mini marshmallows, plus extra for drizzling
10g (¼oz) milk chocolate
1 Oreo biscuit

Serves 🧍🧍🧍🧍🧍🧍🧍🧍🧍🧍 - 🧍🧍

CHEESECAKE & APPLE PIE LOVE CHILD

Apple pie cheesecake, HUH?! Yeah, we've done it! We've stepped right out of the box for this one – apple pie is banging, but so is cheesecake. When it's hard to choose between them, the only answer is a mash-up. You've got the crunchy biscuit base, with the soft cooked apple, topped with creamy cinnamony cheesecake filling, finished off with a shortcrust pastry basket!

Preheat the oven to 180°C (350°F/gas mark 4).

Whizz the digestive biscuits in a processor (or stick 'em in a sandwich bag and bash with a rolling pin). Add the melted butter, and give it a good stir to make sure that all the biscuit is nicely coated, then mix in the cinnamon. Pour into the cake tin (pan), press down gently in the middle to make your base, and push the biscuit up the side to make a wall around the edge of the tin. Level off around the edge with the back of a spoon and place in a freezer for 15 minutes to firm up.

Next make the pastry basket. Line a baking sheet with baking (parchment) paper. Roll out the shortcrust pastry into a rectangle about 20cm (8 inches) by 28cm (11 inches), roughly 2mm (1/8 inch) thick. Cut this into 11 strips (each 20cm/8 inches long and 2.5cm/1 inch wide). Lay these in a woven lattice pattern on the baking sheet. The way to do this is to lay out six of the strips about 1cm (1/2 inch) apart. Then fold every other strip back, almost to the beginning with about 1cm (1/2 inch) overlapping. Lay one strip perpendicular across all the long strips, unfolding the folded strips over the top of it. Then fold every other strip (the ones you haven't done yet) back again as far as the perpendicular strip, and lay a second strip perpendicular after a 1cm (1/2 inch) space, and unfold the strips over the top again. Repeat until you have used up all the strips. Brush with the beaten egg and bake in the oven for 10–12 minutes until golden brown.

For the apple layer, place the chopped apples in a frying pan with the water and butter. Fry for 3 minutes over a medium heat. Add the cornflour (cornstarch), cinnamon and brown sugar, and heat for a further 4 minutes. Pour into a bowl and leave to cool.

To make the filling, beat the cream cheese and sugar together. Add the cinnamon and raisins, and mix thoroughly. Whip the cream to soft peaks and fold it into the mix.

Remove the base from the freezer and spoon in the cooked apples, spreading out evenly. Spoon on the cheese mix, mounding it up slightly in the middle – it can go right up to the edge. Place back in the fridge to firm for 1 hour.

When ready to serve, blitz the digestive biscuit to a fine crumb. Place the pastry basket over the cake, sprinkle with the crumb, brown sugar and raisins, and it's ready!

You'll need: 20cm (8 inch) deep
  springform cake tin (pan)

Base
380g (13 1/2 oz) plain digestive
  biscuits
110g (1/2 cup) unsalted butter, melted
1/2 tsp ground cinnamon

Short crust pastry basket
230g (8oz) ready-made
  shortcrust pastry
1 egg, beaten

Apple layer
490g (1lb 1oz) peeled and roughly
  chopped cooking apples
75ml (scant 1/3 cup) water
45g (3 tbsp) unsalted butter
1 tbsp cornflour (cornstarch)
1 tsp ground cinnamon
80g (scant 1/2 cup) soft brown sugar

Filling
360g (12 3/4 oz) cream cheese
40g (scant 1/4 cup) caster
  (superfine) sugar
1 tsp ground cinnamon
70g (1/2 cup) raisins
100ml (scant 1/2 cup)
  double (heavy) cream

Topping
1 plain digestive biscuit
10g (1 tbsp) soft brown sugar
5g (1/2 tbsp) raisins

Serves 👤👤👤👤👤👤👤👤 - 👤👤

bag of crisps & a pint

BANG BANG

GEEZER & T

MOJITOS

DAQ ATTACK

PROSECCO & STRAWBERRY FLUTES

soho mules

ESPR MAR

Boozy Pleesecakes

ESPRESSO MARTINIS

BAILEYS & WHITE CHOC MINIS

ESPRESSO MARTINIS

From an early age, it's safe to say we've both had a deep love of food. You could tell this by how chubby we were as kids! This love has remained, gaining strength with age. One thing that we both indulge in on a regular basis, is going out for some decent nose bag. We call it a hobby. Trying new foods is up there with the most important things to do in life. So, at the end of a night out, nine courses down, when you need a pick-me-up to get you out of that food coma so that you can go and cut a rug – enter the espresso martini!

Whizz the Amaretti biscuits to a coarse crumb in a food processor (stick 'em in a sandwich bag and bash with a rolling pin if you haven't got a processor). Divide evenly between the glasses, press down gently to make your base and set aside.

Beat the cream cheese and sugar together. Whip the cream until you have stiff peaks and fold it gently into the mix, along with the coffee liqueur and a few drops of black food colouring, until completely combined. Spoon into the glasses, leaving space for the cream topping. Stick 'em in the fridge for at least 3 hours to set.

The cream topping is double simple! Whip the cream to soft peaks, add the vanilla bean paste and mix through. Add to the glasses and level off with a palette knife. Add three coffee beans to each dessert for the authentic martini look. Another win. You know what you're making for dessert for the next dinner party, ay?

You'll need: 2 martini glasses

Base
80g (2³/₄oz) Amaretti biscuits

Filling
150g (²/₃ cup) cream cheese
**20g (1¹/₂ tbsp) caster
  (superfine) sugar**
2 tbsp double (heavy) cream
75ml (scant ¹/₃ cup) coffee liqueur
black food colouring

Topping
**100ml (scant ¹/₂ cup)
  double (heavy) cream**
5ml (1 tsp) vanilla bean paste
6 coffee beans

Serves 👤👤

DAQ ATTACK

You've been given the all clear to go on holiday with the lads, you're buzzing, you get to the airport, everyone else is buzzing, you can barely control your excitement. The flight feels like 3 minutes because you're so excited, taxi (nightmare), hotel, straight into your new holiday clobber, down to the pool bar, what's the first thing you do? Four strawberry daiquiris please, barman!

Whizz the shortbread biscuits to a coarse crumb in a food processor (stick 'em in a sandwich bag and bash with a rolling pin if you haven't got a processor), then spoon through the freeze-dried strawberries. Divide evenly between the glasses, press down gently to make your base and set aside.

Beat the cream cheese and sugar together. Then, add the chopped strawberries, strawberry liqueur and rum to the cream cheese mix and stir together thoroughly. Whip the cream until you have stiff peaks and fold it gently into the cheese mix. Spoon into the glasses. Stick 'em in the fridge for at least 3 hours to set.

Meanwhile, let's crack on with the coulis. Blend the strawberries and sugar in a food processor, it's that simple!

Once the filling is set, remove the glasses from the fridge. Add the fresh strawberries, then a sprinkle of the freeze-dried and finally a drizzle of coulis. A little sprig of mint to make it look like you know what you're doing, and you're done! A simple little dessert that packs a punch!

You'll need: 4 martini glasses

Base
160g (5³/₄oz) shortbread biscuit
2 tbsp freeze-dried strawberries

Filling
70g (¹/₃ cup) cream cheese
10g (2¹/₂ tsp) caster (superfine) sugar
10g (1 tbsp) strawberries, hulled and roughly chopped
15ml (1 tbsp) strawberry liqueur
15ml (1 tbsp) rum
20ml (4 tsp) double (heavy) cream

Strawberry coulis
30g (¹/₃ cup) strawberries, hulled
15g (1¹/₄ tbsp) caster (superfine) sugar

Topping
120g (1¹/₄ cups) strawberries, sliced lengthways
4 tsp freeze-dried strawberries
4 fresh mint sprigs

Serves 🮲🮲🮲🮲

BANG BANG MOJITOS

This one's a summer banger – nothing shouts summer more than a mojito. We've done it again and made your favourite summer bev into a bloody gorgeous cheesecake, for that inevitable BBQ that we'll be having probably only once this year, because that's all the British weather will allow! But still, this pud will make that get-together even more special! Give it a whirl – it won't disappoint!

Whizz your biscuits to a fine crumb in a food processor (stick 'em in a sandwich bag and bash with a rolling pin if you haven't got a processor). Divide evenly between the moulds, press down gently to make your base and set aside.

Beat the cream cheese and caster and brown sugars together. Add the lime zest and juice, along with the rum, and mix together thoroughly. Finely chop the mint leaves (keeping about six whole for decoration) and add to the mix. Whip the cream until you have stiff peaks and fold it gently into the mix.

Dip the whole mint leaves in water and stick them to the inside of the moulds. Spoon in the cheesecake mix, being careful not to remove the mint leaves, and level off with a palette knife. Stick 'em in the fridge for at least 3 hours to set.

Now make the chocolate shards. Line a baking sheet with baking (parchment) paper. Melt the chocolate in the microwave or a heatproof bowl set over a pan of simmering water, then spread it out all over the baking sheet (roughly 2mm/⅛ inch thick). While the chocolate is still wet, sprinkle the finely chopped mint leaves over the top, followed by the peppermint essence. Then whack it in the freezer for 30 minutes to set.

Now it's time to assemble. Remove the chocolate from the freezer and break it up to form shards. Remove the cakes from the fridge and randomly stick in the shards. Blitz the Oreo mint biscuit to a fine crumb, if using, and sprinkle over the top, along with the brown sugar and lime zest. Finish with a sprig of mint on each, if you like. Another simple summer boozy dessert that's going to proper wake up those taste buds!

You'll need: 2 mini cheesecakes moulds or a mini cheesecake tray (12 compartments)

Base
75g (2½oz) Oreo mint biscuits

Filling
200g (scant 1 cup) cream cheese
20g (1⅔ tbsp) caster (superfine) sugar
20g (1¾ tbsp) soft brown sugar
zest and juice of 2 limes
50ml (scant ¼ cup) rum
30g (1oz) fresh mint leaves
40ml (2⅔ tbsp) double (heavy) cream

Chocolate shards
50g (1¾oz) dark chocolate
small handful fresh mint leaves, finely chopped
5ml (1 tsp) peppermint essence

Topping
1 Oreo mint biscuit (optional)
5g (1½ tsp) soft brown sugar
zest of 1 lime
4 small mint sprigs (optional)

Serves 👤👤

BAG OF CRISPS & A PINT

This one came naturally to us and we were buzzing for people to try it. So simple and fun, but booting off in the flavour department! After a day's graft on site, rubbing down 15 door frames, we would consolidate our hard work with a bag of crisps and a guilt-free pint (drink responsibly people)! It was inevitable that we were going to attempt to translate those flavours into a Pleesecake! And, cor blimey, did we? You've gotta give this one a go. It's a proper geezer-sized canapé for any sort of get-together!

You'll need: 8 double shot glasses (so it looks like little pints of lager!)

Base

4 packets of crisps (about 100g/3½oz) – we recommend ridged crisps for stability
1 smoked bacon rasher (slice)

Jelly filling

60ml (¼ cup) water
60g (⅓ cup) sugar
2 sheets gelatine
120ml (½ cup) beer – we recommend a good-quality beer or ale

Topping

40g (1½oz) goat's cheese

Serves 

First of all, we wanna get this beer jelly on the go, so get a saucepan and bring the water to the boil. Line a small rectangular dish (at least 2.5cm/1 inch deep) with cling film (plastic wrap).

Put your sugar and gelatine sheets into the water and stir until completely dissolved. Once dissolved, take the pan off the heat and pour the beer into the saucepan and give it a good old stir (save the surplus beer for sneaky swigs). Once thoroughly stirred, pour the jelly mix into the prepared dish (ideally you want the jelly 2.5–4cm/1–1½ inches thick). Get it in the fridge and let it set for 2 hours.

Smash the bags of crisps until you have a nice coarse crumb, and put a tablespoon into the bottom of each glass to create your base. Cook the bacon under the grill (broiler) for 8–10 minutes (depending on the level of crispiness you like), chop it up and add to the base.

Use a spare shot glass as a cutter and cut out eight little cylinders of jelly that perfectly fit each glass. Gently slide the beer jellies on top of the crisp-and-bacon bases.

Crumble up the goat's cheese and press it in on top of the jelly to form the beer topper. Now, if this doesn't impress your friends, I don't know what will!

SOHO MULES

A couple of our pals were members of the Soho House group (cutla memberships please, if you're reading Soho House people). We'd be their plus three on their membership and rinse the bar of these banging drinks called Soho Mules. Stem ginger, vodka and ginger ale – an all-year-round tipple. Getting all our favourite flavours into this book was challenging, but we did it. This one's a corker, promise! If you like ginger, you're going to love this Pleesecake! So, so simple!

Whizz the ginger nut biscuits to a fine crumb in a food processor (stick 'em in a sandwich bag and bash with a rolling pin if you haven't got a processor). Add the melted butter, and give it a good stir to make sure that all the biscuit is nicely coated, then mix in the citrus zest. Divide equally between the moulds, press down gently to make your base and place in the fridge for 30 minutes to firm up.

Beat the cream cheese and sugar together. Add the lime zest and juice, along with the ginger paste, crystallized ginger and vodka, and mix together thoroughly. Whip the cream until you have stiff peaks and fold it gently into the mix. Spoon into the moulds and level off with a palette knife. Stick 'em back in the fridge for at least 3 hours to set.

Once set, remove from the fridge and take them out of the moulds. The topping is double easy. Simply spike the stem ginger and crystallized ginger on a cocktail stick (toothpick) and dig into the cakes. Blitz the ginger nut biscuit to a fine crumb and sprinkle over the top. A few leaves of fresh mint finish this little beaut off!

You'll need: 2 mini cheesecake moulds or a mini cheesecake tray (12 compartments)

Base
75g (2³⁄₄oz) ginger nut biscuits
20g (1¹⁄₂ tbsp) unsalted butter, melted
zest of ¹⁄₂ lemon
zest of 1 lime

Filling
200g (scant 1 cup) cream cheese
50g (¹⁄₄ cup) caster (superfine) sugar
zest and juice of 1 lime
1 tsp ginger paste
20g (³⁄₄oz) crystallized ginger
60ml (¹⁄₄ cup) vodka
80ml (¹⁄₃ cup) double (heavy) cream

Topping
40g (1¹⁄₂oz) stem ginger, cut into small pieces
10g (¹⁄₄oz) crystallized ginger, cut into small pieces
1 ginger nut biscuit
small handful of fresh mint leaves

Serves ♟♟

GEEZER & T

During the summer, there's nothing more refreshing than an ice-cold gin and tonic! Many a blurry night has been had on these. It's our tipple during the summer months, not that we have summer months. More like warmer winter months. Anyway, we've turned our summer bevy into a lovely refreshing cheesecake that is bound to go down a treat whatever the weather! Any plonker can make these, so no excuses!

Whizz the Viennese biscuits to a fine crumb in a food processor (stick 'em in a sandwich bag and bash with a rolling pin if you haven't got a processor). Add the melted butter, and give it a good stir to make sure that all the biscuit is nicely coated, then mix in the citrus zest. Divide evenly between the tumblers, press down gently to make your base and place in the fridge for 30 minutes to firm up.

Beat the cream cheese and sugar together. Add the citrus zest and juice and the gin, and mix together thoroughly. Whip the cream until you have stiff peaks and fold it gently into the mix. A silky-smooth texture is what you're going for here! Spoon into the tumblers. Stick 'em back in the fridge for at least 3 hours to set.

To make the gel, pour the lemon juice and water into a saucepan and add the sugar and agar agar or gelatine powder. Heat over a low to medium heat until the sugar has dissolved. Turn up the heat and bring to the boil. Remove from the heat and add the gin. Stir well and pour into a shallow dish. Cool for at least 2 hours.

When you're ready to decorate, spoon the gel into a piping bag and pipe small dollops randomly on the cheesecakes. Blitz the Viennese biscuit to a fine crumb and sprinkle over the top. Add a final sprinkling of lemon and lime zest and you're ready to serve! You're going to love this one during the summer!

You'll need: 2 small glass tumblers

Base
80g (2³/₄oz) lemon cream
  Viennese biscuits
12g (³/₄ tbsp) unsalted butter, melted
zest of 1 lemon
zest of 1 lime

Filling
200g (scant 1 cup) cream cheese
40g (scant ¹/₄ cup) caster
  (superfine) sugar
zest and juice of 1 lemon
zest and juice of 1 lime
50ml (scant ¹/₄ cup) gin
40ml (2²/₃ tbsp) double
  (heavy) cream

Lemon and gin gel
125ml (¹/₂ cup) lemon juice
125ml (¹/₂ cup) water
50g (¹/₄ cup) caster (superfine) sugar
1 tsp agar agar or gelatine powder
40ml (2²/₃ tbsp) gin

Topping
1 lemon cream Viennese biscuit
zest of 1 lemon
zest of 1 lime

Serves

BAILEYS & WHITE CHOC MINIS

This recipe is slightly seasonal perhaps, but we don't care and think it can be enjoyed any time of the year! This Pleesecake is so creamy and decadent it's going to win you over in the first mouthful. It's what a proper dessert should taste like, no messing around here. When you eat this, you know it's dessert time!

Whizz the biscuits to a fine crumb in a food processor (stick 'em in a sandwich bag and bash with a rolling pin if you haven't got a processor). Add the melted butter, and give it a good stir to make sure that all the biscuit is nicely coated, then mix in the choc drops. Divide evenly between the moulds, press down gently to make your base and place in the fridge for 30 minutes to firm up.

Beat the cream cheese and sugar together. Melt the white chocolate (not the drops) in a heatproof bowl set over a pan of simmering water. Add the Baileys and melted white chocolate to the cheese and mix together thoroughly. Whip the cream until you have stiff peaks and fold it gently into the mix, along with the white choc drops. Spoon into the moulds and level off with a palette knife. Stick 'em in the freezer for at least 3 hours to set.

Once firm, remove from the freezer, take them out of the moulds and they're ready to decorate. Melt the topping white chocolate as above and spoon onto each cake. While the chocolate is still wet, add the creamy fudge and the mini fudge pieces, and dot with clotted cream.

Some seriously indulgent flavours are going on here! You ain't going to be sharing this with anyone! Fact!

Allow to defrost in the fridge for 1–2 hours before serving.

You'll need: 4 mini cheesecake moulds or a mini cheesecake tray (12 compartments)

Base
120g (4¼oz) plain digestive biscuits
30g (2 tbsp) unsalted butter, melted
40g (1½oz) white chocolate drops

Filling
400g (14oz) cream cheese
80g (generous ⅓ cup) caster (superfine) sugar
45g (1½oz) white chocolate
100ml (scant ½ cup) Baileys
160ml (⅔ cup) double (heavy) cream
40g (1½oz) white chocolate drops

Topping
60g (2¼oz) white chocolate
60g (2¼oz) creamy fudge, cut into small pieces
20g (¾oz) mini fudge pieces
115g (4oz) clotted cream

Serves

PROSECCO & STRAWBERRY FLUTES

Fellas, hear us out – if you can't be seen eating a pretty little dessert out of a champagne flute, don't worry – you can whack this in a pint glass if that makes you feel more comfortable. The taste will win you over and you won't care what you're eating this from at the end of the day. In the unlikely event that any of this dessert ends up on the floor somewhere, we still endorse eating it, given that it would be too much of a waste otherwise! Ladies, we all know you love a glass of bubbly, now we've smashed together cheesecake and Prosecco and cor blimey, does it work! Summer banger right here!

Whizz the shortbread biscuits to a fine crumb in a food processor (stick 'em in a sandwich bag and bash with a rolling pin if you haven't got a processor), then stir through the freeze-dried strawberries. Divide evenly between the champagne flutes, press down gently to make your base and set aside.

Beat the cream cheese and sugar together. Add the Prosecco (also known as pro-psycho as it has a tendency to make people go crazy) and the chopped strawberries and mix together thoroughly. Whip the cream until you have soft peaks and fold it gently into the mix. Spoon into the glasses. Stick 'em in the fridge for at least 3 hours to set, while you get on with the final bits.

For the coulis, simply blend the strawberries and sugar in a food processor.

Once the filling is set, remove the glasses from the fridge and slide one strawberry onto the edge of each glass. Sprinkle with the freeze-dried strawberries and some white choc drops, and give it a healthy drizzle of coulis. Finito! Get involved, these ones boooottttt offfffff!

Serves

You'll need: 2 champagne flutes

Base
60g (2¼oz) shortbread biscuits
2 tbsp freeze-dried strawberries

Filling
120g (½ cup) cream cheese
12g (1 tbsp) caster (superfine) sugar
100ml (scant ½ cup) Prosecco
40g (scant ½ cup) fresh
   strawberries, hulled and
   finely chopped
40ml (2⅔ tbsp) double
   (heavy) cream

Strawberry coulis
40g (¼ cup) fresh strawberries
10g (¾ tbsp) caster
   (superfine) sugar

Topping
2 fresh strawberries
1 tbsp freeze-dried strawberries
10g (¼oz) white chocolate drops

DOUBLE CHOCOLATE PLEESE SHAKE

BANANA & SALTED CAZZA PLEESE SHAKE

guilt-free pleeseshake

STR

& SWEETS

Pleeseshakes

AWBERRY
EESESHAKE

DOUBLE CHOCOLATE PLEESESHAKE

Pleeseshakes? Cheesecake milkshakes? Yes! Cheesecake milkshakes!!! These are real fun to make and if you're not in the mood for making a full cheesecake and only have 5 minutes to come up with a dessert, these are the recipes for you! Now, get involved. We want to see some of your pleeseshakes, so get posting and tagging – #pleeseshakes.

Whizz up the biscuits to a coarse crumb in a food processor (stick 'em in a sandwich bag and bash with a rolling pin if you haven't got a processor). Divide evenly between the serving glasses, along with the choc chips.

Blend all the filling ingredients for 2 minutes and pour into the glasses.

Topping wise, we've suggested a few but we recommend adding more if we haven't suggested enough! Swirl on a drizzle of chocolate sauce. If using the brownie cookies, blitz them to a fine crumb in the processor and sprinkle over the top of the shake. Add some chocolate chips, if you like.

You'll need: 2 serving glasses

Base
80g (2³/₄oz) double chocolate
   digestive biscuits
10g (¹/₄oz) milk chocolate chips
10g (¹/₄oz) dark chocolate chips

Filling
100ml (scant ¹/₂ cup) double
   (heavy) cream
100ml (scant ¹/₂ cup) full-fat
   (whole) milk
100g (¹/₃ cup) chocolate or
   chocolate hazelnut spread
300g (10¹/₂oz) chocolate ice cream
120g (4¹/₄oz) chocolate brownie
180g (³/₄ cup) cream cheese

Topping (suggested)
chocolate sauce – 10-second
   no-break drizzle!
120g (4¹/₄oz) chocolate brownie
double choc chip cookies – loads
20g (³/₄oz) milk chocolate chips
20g (³/₄oz) dark chocolate chips

Serves

BANANA & SALTED CAZZA PLEESESHAKE

We challenge you to find a better flavour for a milkshake! This one is so good it'll send you into a foodgasm on your first sip! Our shake range is one of our favourite sections, just for the fact that they taste amazing, take about 2 seconds to make and are a great alternative to a dessert if you're looking for something special, quick and easy!

Whizz up the biscuits to a coarse crumb in a food processor (stick 'em in a sandwich bag and bash with a rolling pin if you haven't got a processor). Divide evenly between the serving glasses.

Blend all the filling ingredients for 2 minutes and pour into the glasses.

A squirt of squirty cream and a sprinkle of some creamy fudge pieces, banana chips and a lengthy drizzle of caramel sauce! UNBELIEVABLE!

You'll need: 2 serving glasses

Base
80g (2³/₄oz) double chocolate
 digestive biscuits

Filling
100ml (scant ¹/₂ cup) double
 (heavy) cream
70g (¹/₄ cup) salted caramel sauce
875ml (3³/₄ cups) salted caramel
 ice cream
150g (5¹/₂oz) banana
180g (³/₄ cup) cream cheese
30g (¹/₃ cup) banana chips
20g (³/₄oz) mini fudge pieces
100ml (scant ¹/₂ cup) semi-skimmed
 (reduced-fat 2%) milk
10ml (2 tsp) banana essence
¹/₂ tsp sea salt

Topping (suggested)
squirty cream – as much as
 you can fit on
20g (³/₄oz) mini fudge pieces
a few banana chips (optional)
caramel sauce – 5-second
 no-break dribble!

Serves

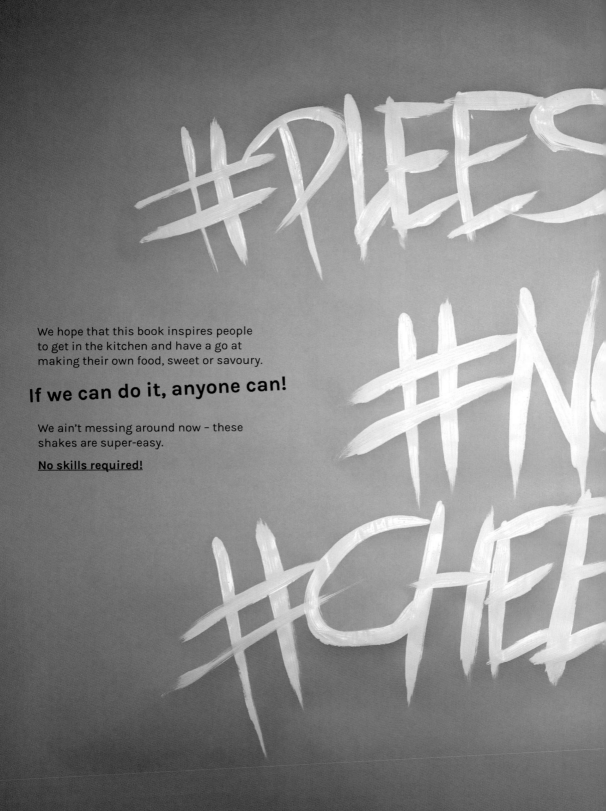

We hope that this book inspires people to get in the kitchen and have a go at making their own food, sweet or savoury.

If we can do it, anyone can!

We ain't messing around now – these shakes are super-easy.

No skills required!

ECAKES

OT

SECAKES

SECAKES

STRAWBERRY & SWEETS PLEESESHAKE

We've all got a childish side locked away, but with this pick 'n' mix cheesecake milkshake, your inner kid will be coming out to play for sure! And if you're a child, your inner kid is already out because, well, you're a child! Anyway, the nostalgia of pick 'n' mix sweets still lives on with us, and you can't beat a pink foam shrimp, an ice cream marshmallow or a milk bottle. Smashing it on a cheesecake milkshake makes it that much better! Enjoy!

Whizz the biscuits to a coarse crumb in a food processor (stick 'em in a sandwich bag and bash with a rolling pin if you haven't got a processor). Divide evenly between the glasses and add the jelly tots.

Blend all the filling ingredients for 2 minutes and pour into the glasses.

To top, melt some white chocolate in a microwave or heatproof bowl over a pan of simmering water and drizzle around the inside and outside of the rim of the glass. Pour in the shake mixture. Add a guilty mound of squirty cream, and stick the topping ingredients to the cream and white chocolate.

A final drizzle of strawberry sauce and you've just won the milkshake competition!

You'll need: 2 serving glasses

Base
80g (2³/₄oz) plain digestive biscuits
30g (1oz) jelly tots

Filling
100ml (scant ¹/₂ cup) double (heavy) cream
100ml (scant ¹/₂ cup) full-fat (whole) milk
300g (10¹/₂oz) strawberry ice cream
180g (³/₄ cup) cream cheese
200g (2 cups) strawberries
200g (²/₃ cup) strawberry jam

Toppings
white chocolate
squirty cream
sprinkles
pick 'n' mix sweets
strawberries, halved lengthways
strawberry sauce

Serves

GUILT-FREE PLEESESHAKE

We love our indulgent pleeseshakes, they're so easy to make and take no time at all! But naturally, we've had to balance out this section with a healthy shake, having already created three double-guilty ones. We haven't scrimped on flavours though. Lovely and fruity, with real healthy natural ingredients! This is great for breakfast or as a healthy dessert option mid-week. Banging!

For the base, simply pour the oats and mixed seeds into a serving glasses.

Now blend all the filling ingredients for 2–3 minutes. Pour into the glasses and top with a spoonful of Greek yogurt, a drizzle of honey and a sprinkle of mixed seeds. Simple and so decent!

You'll need: 2 serving glasses

Base
80g (³/₄ cup) oats
20g (³/₄oz) mixed seeds

Filling
400ml (scant 1²/₃ cups) almond milk
100g (scant ½ cup) light cream cheese
120g (4¼oz) avocado
70g (generous ⅓ cup) pitted dates
20g (³/₄oz) chia seeds
90g (3oz) raspberries
90g (3oz) pineapple
2 cups ice

Topping
80g (scant ½ cup) Greek yogurt
2 tbsp honey
30g (¼ cup) mixed seeds

Serves

BRENDON'S ACKNOWLEDGEMENTS

I would firstly like to say thank you to my man Joe for giving me the opportunity in raising this company and writing the book with him.

Big up the BC for the shoutouts and the following it's created.

Holdtight Anna and the team at Madeleine Milburn for spotting us and giving us the amazing chance to do this book.

I want to thank my wife for putting up with me and being sweet with not seeing me for the last year.

And finally big up the guys at Quadrille for taking us painters/geezers on and giving us the chance to produce this bestseller. Without all of you lot this wouldn't have been possible. Holdtight book two... soon come.

JOE'S ACKNOWLEDGEMENTS

The last 16 months have been, what I can only describe as the hardest, most testing 16 months of our lives. The response and reaction people have had to Pleesecakes has been pretty mad!

From decorating houses to decorating cakes was never a plan! But Brendon and I have had a year we'll never forget. The team at Madeleine Milburn and the team at Quadrille have turned an idea into a bloody book!

We still can't believe we've written a book! So THANK YOU to Sarah, Claire, Amy and everyone at Quadrille, you're all quality! Big THANK YOU to Madeleine, Anna, Giles, Hayley and everyone at Madeleine Milburn. Thanks to Kris Kirkham for his ridiculous photography and Louie and Tamara for making all the recipes look double delicious!! BIG UP YEAH!

Big shout out to my family, for helping grow this business – we had my dad, sister and mum all out on deliveries at one point! (Mum still does most of the deliveries!) Big up my bird Ellie, always there with mad support and encouragement! Mad love to you all!

Obviously the social media following and support has been RIDICULOUS, again, wouldn't have been possible without you all!

I hope you've all enjoyed the book and taken something away from it! Let us know if you want books two, three, four and five and we'll smash them out for you!

HOLDTIGHT!!!!!

 @pleesecakes

www.pleesecakes.com